SOME 411 OF GOD

And God Said

RON FRAZIER

authorHOUSE

AuthorHouse™
1663 Liberty Drive
Bloomington, IN 47403
www.authorhouse.com
Phone: 1 (800) 839-8640

Published by AuthorHouse 10/30/2018

ISBN: 978-1-5462-6662-4 (sc)
ISBN: 978-1-5462-6663-1 (e)

ABOUT THE AUTHOR

After God has so Graciously Blessed me and has given me the opportunity to learn more about His Word, and about how His Kingdom Principles work and operate in this world and in our lives, and also understanding more about His Grace and His Love for us, it has made a tremendous and lasting impact in my life and in the lives of those close to me.

He has also helped me to understand our God Given Authority that He has given us as a born again believer over Satan and all his evil.

Luke 10:19

Jesus taught and preached about The Kingdom Of God and about how the principles of The Kingdom operated in this world by us having and using our Faith In God and His Word.

He taught us that if we will truly understand how the Spiritual Laws Of God works, especially The Law Of Faith, that it could change our lives. He showed us how The Law Of Faith operates and how the Power and the Authority of it will take control and dominion over all other things.

He taught us and told us that when we speak our faith out of our mouth and truly believe in our heart and have no doubt in that what we are saying will happen, that those things we say will manifest in our lives.

Mark 11:23

It is indeed a life changing, peaceful, and powerful experience. I was at one time just as anyone else who had feelings of doubt and unbelief. But when I heard some teaching on who we are to God and who He is to us, I began to study His Word and started to truly understand about His Love, about His Unconditional Love for us, and what His Gift of Grace was really about. And when I really got hold of this and fully received His Love, things began to change in my perspective of life. My fellowship with my Father God in Heaven increased and He started revealing things to me in His Word and by His Holy Spirit.

Over a period of time, the things talked about in this book were some of the things that has been revealed to me by His Love and by His Grace. He helped me in the renewing of my mind to see things as He sees them and to do and to think on things the way He thinks and does them. My everyday life, my everyday practices, and my everyday conduct are in the pages of this book.

He taught me the difference in understanding our self-righteousness and His Righteousness, that we are only made righteous through the Blood Of Jesus. And when He sees us as His children, He sees us through the Righteousness of Jesus. Our performance and our conduct does not determine our being made right with God, it is only because of what Jesus did and our believing and receiving Jesus as our Saviour and Lord that makes us right with Him.

He made it perfectly clear that my sins have already been forgiven and when I make a mistake and/or commit a sin, that I was to repent and turn from it and confess it to Him, He has already forgiven it and forgotten about it because of what Jesus has already done. And because He loves me and wants to have fellowship with me, He would not condemn me and that I don't need to condemn myself but to receive my forgiveness from Him and continue to have our fellowship together. He taught me not to let Satan condemn me either. My sins have been forgiven and that all my past sins are none of Satan's business.

He has helped me understand that we as born again believers have Authority over Satan and all his demonic activity. Satan has no authority over us unless we give it to him by the ways talked about in this book. I've seen healing take place when I have layed hands on someone in Jesus Name. I've seen situations change by speaking faith to it. I've seen the Power of Our Words at work. THIS IS REAL !!! Grab hold of it, in the Precious Holy Name Of Jesus.

INTRODUCTION AND
OPENING STATEMENT

Some of the things you are about to read may seem to be way out there, and may even seem to some as being nothing more than foolish and radical statements.

But just because a person may have a lack of understanding or a lack of wisdom about the character and goodness of God, that does not affect or change the way God truly is. God has made the statement Himself about why people perish. He said "my people perish due to the lack of knowledge."

It is the knowledge and wisdom of God that He so graciously and mercifully gifts to His people, through His Word, and His Holy Spirit, and revelation knowledge, that will result in ultimately changing the circumstances in a persons life.

And just because these principles and statements that are talked about in this book are not common everyday practice by very many people, and they are not fully understood by many, it does not change the fact that they are the truth. And as the Word of God says, "you shall know the truth and the truth shall set you free."

Jesus, The Christ, is our truth. He has redeemed us from the curse of the law and He has set us born again believers free from "the law of sin and death." and has given us believers the victory over death. He has delivered us from the afflictions and of the oppression of our enemy Satan, and He has suffered for us and He bore our sickness and pain so that we would not have to.

The completed work of Jesus, our Lord, before and during and after His suffering on the Cross, has already made all the things talked about in this book available to us. There is nothing else due and nothing else that has to be done because it has all been completed and has already been paid in full.

All that is required now is for us to do our part. We must actually and truthfully believe what God has said and the promises that He has made to us. We must believe and come to the absolute understanding that God really and truly cares about us and that He truly and absolutely loves us unconditionally.

He is not a God who sits and waits for us to do something wrong and then jumps on us with some type of curse or sickness to punish us or teach us a lesson. He is our loving and caring Father in Heaven.

You are precious and loved by God and He wants you to have the very best life that you can possibly have while you live here in this world.

He wants you to experience His love and grace toward you in your everyday life until it is time for you to be with Him in heaven.

The more you focus on what Jesus and our Father in Heaven has done for us, the more you will experience His Divine Love and His ever present help in every part of your life. I know that I have, and it is a wonderful and peaceful experience.

Always, and I say again, always, keep a grateful heart to God for what He has done and always give reverence and respect and honor to God and His Word for this is the fear of The Lord and the beginning of wisdom and knowledge.

I know since I have gotten this revelation of knowledge that God so lovingly and gracefully has granted to me and has blessed me with this understanding, that He wants others to share in this blessing as well.

When I began to truly and fully trust God, I began to see things change in my life and I have had that peace which surpasses all understanding everyday and have seen the Faithfulness of God at work in my life and in the life of others.

I pray that you will immerse yourself in the writings in this book and see God's love and mercy for us, and experience an abundance of His healing and His restoration power through the words of His 411 information that has been supplied to us by His loving and merciful grace.

Be careful and be serious about how you hear and use these words in this book for they are The Word Of God, the true living Word Of God, and they are not only just words on paper, but they are life to your body, your soul, and your spirit.

May the Grace Of God bless you, keep you, and prosper you in all things. And may the information that has been made available to you in this book through the Grace of God and His Love for us, richly bless you with more of our needed understanding of God's Word, the spiritual laws of the spirit realm, and the Promises Of God. If you will take this book and all of its teaching seriously and put it into your everyday practice in your daily life, using your God given faith, it will change your life, for I know it has in mine.

CONTENTS

CHAPTER 1

BORN TWICE, NEVER DIE OR BORN ONCE, DIE TWICE

I know the first part of this chapter may be nothing new, but bear with me because I need to include this to help explain the contents of the chapter and how all of it will come together.

When all of us are born our natural birth, we all have a spirit in us from the time of creation. (Genesis 2:7) "And the Lord formed Man from the dust of the earth, and breathed into the nostrils of the man the breath of life, and man became a living soul." A living creature, an individual complete with a body, soul, and spirit.

God said let us create man in our own image, just as God has three parts, The Father, The Son, and The Holy Spirit, so it is with humans, body, soul, and spirit.

The Apostle Paul wrote in (1 Thessolonians 5:23) "Now may the God of Peace Himself sanctify you entirely and may your spirit and soul and body be presented complete, without blame at the coming of our Lord Jesus Christ."

Man is made up of tangible material and intangible material. The body can be seen and touched and is necessary to live in this physical world and cannot live in the spiritual world. The soul is your will, your mind, and your emotions. Your spirit is who you really are, the life in you.

The spirit and soul life span exists beyond the physical life span of the body and it is the spirit part of you, who you really are, that will live for eternity in either Heaven or Hell.

You received your spirit when God breathed life into man at creation and it has been passed on from generation to generation.

God is a Spirit (John 4:24) and when He breathed into man, He breathed in His Spirit.

Adam was created perfect in the likeness and Spirit of God until he disobeyed God and committed sin in the Garden Of Eden and his spirit became corrupt and no longer pure with God's Spirit. And it was for that reason that the human spirit and God's Spirit were separated from each other, and the human spirit did not bear witness with God's Spirit any longer because it became dead to sin. As a result of this, we were all born with a sinful spirit.

But when God sent His Son, Jesus, who sometimes is called the "second man" and also the "last Adam" God had made a way for us to be reconciled to Him because of what He did for us on The Cross.

The Bible calls Jesus the "last Adam" and the "second man" in Paul's writing in the book of Corinthians.

(1 Corinthians 15: 45-48) "So it is written: the first man Adam became a living being; the last Adam was made a living spirit. The spiritual did not come first, but the natural, and after that the spiritual. The first man was from the dust of the earth, the second man from heaven. As was the earthly man, so are those who are of the earth, and is the man from heaven, so also are those who are from heaven."

Because Adam sinned, the natural state of humans at natural birth is that of humans with a fallen nature and a sinful dead spirit toward God. But because the Lord Jesus is the last Adam and the second man, He is the last man to be without a sin nature. His nature was both human and divine. He was the second man, the man from heaven.

As the God-man without sin, He was the suitable sacrafice from God for the sins of the world and Jesus offered Himself as the sacrafice for sin.

When a person realizes that there is a need in their life for a Saviour and they come to believe, truly believe, that they need a personal relationship and a personal fellowship with their Heavenly Father and they accept Jesus as their Lord and Saviour and God's gift of Grace and receive their forgiveness of sin from God, their spirit is revived, brought to life, and born again.

God sends His Spirit to live in them, and seals them with His Holy Spirit, and claims them for His own. He seals them with His Spirit as a Promise of the gift of eternal life and their eternal redemption and they will never die a spiritual death and will not be seperated from Him again.

When a person dies their natural death, their spirit, who they really are, will go to be present with the Lord and they will never feel death. The very moment your physical body dies, your spirit will leave your body and go to be present with the Lord Jesus in Paradise if you are born again. Your body will lay in the grave until the Resurrection Of Life when the Rapture takes place. We will talk more about this later when we will talk about The Judgement.

We can not say the same for a person who never received salvation and accepted Jesus as their Saviour. We will talk about that later as well.

Being born again, that spiritual re-birth by us believing in Jesus.

Jesus told Martha, the sister of Lazurus, that He was the resurrection and the life.

(John 11: 25-26) "I am the resurrection and the life: he that believes in me, though he was dead (spiritually dead) yet shall he live: and whosoever liveth and believes in me (born again) shall never die."

Im sure we have all heard (John 3:16) and we know that it is true, and I trust that you know about what happened at the Cross, and thank God and our Lord Jesus for it. So now I am going to talk about what happened between the time that Jesus was placed in the tomb and His resurrection.

While Jesus was here walking on the earth, He walked as a man in the flesh just as we are, but He had the fullness of God's Holy Spirit inside of Him leading and telling Him what to say and do, He was a God-man. He also was a human man with a body, soul, and spirit, just as we are.

When He died on the Cross, His spirit left His body, just as a born again believers spirit does. His spirit went to Hades/Paradise. But He was also God and because of it, He was able to strip Satan of all his authority over mankind that he stole from Adam in the garden and later delegated that authority back to born again believers, the children of God, where God meant for it to be.

He took the keys to Hell, death, and the grave away from Satan, which gave us who believe victory over death. He moved Paradise to the third heaven where God is and led the saints of old time that were there to the new Paradise.

You may find it surprising that Paradise was in Hades but Jesus spoke of it when He told the story of the Rich man and Lazurus in (Luke 16: 19-31) He said that the Rich man was in Hades (Torment) and Lazurus, the beggar, was in the Bosom of Abraham (Paradise) and there was a great gulf between the two preventing anyone from crossing over to the other side. One side was for those who died in sin and belonged to Satan and the other side for those who died as believers in God and belonged to God.

Then later in the New Testament, in 2 Corinthians, after the Resurrection of Jesus, Paul tells us of him being called up to the third heavens, to Paradise, whether in the body or out of the body, he wasn't sure, where he heard inexpressable words, which is not lawful for men to say or utter.(2 Corinthians 12: 2-4) This shows that Paradise was indeed moved. Paul tells us that Jesus descended into the lower parts of the earth before ascending into heaven(Ephesians 4:9-10) and Jesus tells us that He took the keys to Hades and death in (Revelations 1:18) "I am He who lives and was dead, and behold, I am alive forevermore. And I have the keys of Hades and Death."

After all this, God raised Jesus from the dead and He received His Glorified Body. A body that can live in the physical world and in the spiritual world, a body we will receive when Jesus comes to Rapture His people.

Knowing that all scripture is given by the inspiration of the Holy Spirit Of God, It is safe to say that Paradise exists, Hell exists, Jesus moved Paradise, stripped Satan of his authority over mankind, took the keys to Hell, death, and the grave, gave us believers victory over death, and promised that if we would believe and accept Jesus as our Saviour, that we would never taste death but we would live forever.

So if you are born a natural birth and have been reborn in your spirit, born twice, you will never die. Your physical body will die, but your spirit will never die.

Our physical body, if we should have our physical death before the Rapture, will lay in the grave until the Rapture and it is then we will receive our Glorified Bodies. Our spirit will be with Jesus when He comes and be re-united with our body which will be raised incorruptable, perfect, and glorified. Those that are still alive and are born again shall be called up and changed just as those bodies that were dead.

(1 Corinthians 15:52) "It will happen in a moment, in the blink of an eye, when the last trumpet is blown. For when the trumpet sounds, those who have died will be raised imperishable to live forever. And we who are living will also be transformed."

It will be a body like Jesus has so we will be able to reign with Him when Heaven is moved to earth. Be able to live in a spiritual or physical world. (Revelation 21: 1-7)

Unless spiritual death is reversed in this life, the end result will be eternal death. Eternal death or the second death is an ultimate form of eternal seperation from God. Once a person has experienced this "second death" there is no hope for them.

Remember that I have stated in this chapter that your spirit will never die but will live eternally. How awlful it would be to be in eternal torment knowing that there is no hope, no relief, and no way of changing your circumstances.

When your body dies the physical death and your spirit has never been redeemed by the Grace Of God, and you never accepted Jesus, that is exactly the consequences of what will happen. This condition is known as "The second death"

When you die your physical death and your spirit leaves your body, this is your first death. If you are not saved, your spirit will go to Hades (Torment), where the Rich man was and still is today and will remain until The Great White Throne Judgement Of God takes place.

There are two resurrections, The Resurrection Of Life (1 Thessolonians 4:16) this is the resurrection for those that have been saved, The Rapture, and this takes place before the 1000 year reign of Christ. The second is The Resurrection Of The Damned Or Condemnation (John 5:29) this is for those who never got saved and it takes place at the end of the 1000 year reign. These are those that will appear before The Great White Throne Judgement.

There is 3 stages of The Resurrection Of Life. The first was when Jesus was crucified and there was an earthquake and many of the Old Testament Saints graves were opened and they were raised (Matthew 27: 51-52) The second is the one already mentioned, The Rapture, and the third and final is after the Rapture and Tribulation period. These are the ones who got saved after the Rapture and did not take the Mark Of The Beast and were killed because they would not swear an alliegance to the anti-christ. These are the ones resurrected just before Christ comes to earth with the New Heaven to reign for a thousand years.

During that thousand year reign, God will bind up Satan, and afterward will loose him for a season to rebel against God again, and when that season is over, God will be done with Satan when He casts him into the lake of fire and brimstone (Hell).

But the doom of Satan is not the end of it all, there is still the judgement of those unbelievers and rejectors of God whose bodies are still in the grave and their spirits are in torment. Those who never got saved or born again, who were only born through a natural birth and never through a spiritual birth, born once.

They have already died once, but now they await their second death, The Great White Throne Judgement. The Judge is our Lord Jesus Christ Himself. (John 5: 22) "The Father judgeth no man, but has assigned all judgement to the Son."

It is here where Jesus will sit in judgement of all the ones who hated, rejected, and refused to acknowledge Him. They payed no attention to the love of God and what Jesus did for them on the Cross. They remained dead in their sins and never repented. They remained spiritually dead and having no eternal life, yet they are standing before God physically alive in their resurrected body about to receive their final sentence from the Son of God. They are about to be cast into Hell.

(Revelation 20: 11-15) "From every part of the earth the bodies of the unbelievers were raised, the sea gave up the dead which were in it, and death and Hades delivered up the dead which were in them and they were judged every man according to their works."

They will be forever banished from the presence of God and have eternal punishment in the Lake Of Fire (Hell).

Thank God, and Glory Be To God, that there will be not one single born again believer, truly born again, standing before the judgement of The Great White Throne.

It will be only the unsaved and by their own personal choice of rejecting the sacrafice that Jesus made for us on the Cross and their refusing to accept Him as their Lord and Saviour that will put them there. Their unbelief and refusal to receive the gift of God's grace and His mercy will forever seal their fate.

How awlful it will be for them to be as this chapter title says, Born Once, Die Twice." Father God, help us to reach the lost souls and help us to bring them to You so that You shall give them mercy and they may be reconciled to You. In Jesus Name we pray and ask these things." Amen.

CHAPTER 2

OUR NEED FOR SALVATION
AND UNDERSTANDING

After reading the first chapter of this book, are you concerned about your future?

If you are truly a Christian born again believer, rejoice and be glad. If you are not saved and see that you are in need of a Saviour, and want a relationship with Jesus and God our Father in heaven, this chapter can help you to obtain this most important thing in your life.

The decision you make about this can not only determine where you will spend eternity but will also determine the quality and destiny of your life here on earth.

Remember what I have written in chapter 1 about the state of our spirit when we are born at natural birth. That should send up a red flag to us all. We should realize immediately that we need a Saviour, someone to save us from eternal damnation, someone to save us from Satan and his demonic activity, someone we can trust, someone who truly loves us. and that someone is The Lord Jesus Christ and His Father in heaven.

It makes no difference how good a person is or of all the good things they do. We can never be good enough or do enough good things in our own efforts in order to be righteous, the right standing with God, according to His standards.

God knew we could not do it on our own because that had been proven with Adam in The Garden Of Eden and had been passed on from generation to generation. And sin offering were offered up to God every year by The Priests for their sins and the sins of the people. These animal sacrafices only covered their sin and did not take them away. The God given authority that was stolen from Adam in the garden was still in the possession of Satan and God was not happy with this.

He needed a suitable and perfect sacrafice to take sins away and not only cover them as the animal sacrafices did. He did not take pleasure in this type of sacrafice every year and wanted to do away with it. He needed to get back that authority Satan had stolen and give it back to mankind where He placed it at the beginning. And that is why He sent His Son Jesus to accomplish these things and to save us from our eternal seperation from Him and an eternity of torment and destruction. He needed to have a sacrafice for eternal redemption and Jesus was that sacrafice.

One of the first things a person should know is how much God really loves them. Some people never actually realize of just how much He truly loves us and cares for us. In addition to not knowing this, some people do not truly understand the will of God for their life or who they are, their indentity, in the body of Christ and God's Family.

It is my hope and prayer that this chapter will help them understand these things and I pray His Holy Spirit will help them understand what God The Father, God The Son, and God the Holy Spirit wants them to know.

It is my intentions in this and the following chapters of this book to help people to understand what it means to be saved, born again, to have understanding of how much God loves and cares for them, their indentity in God's Family, and their God given authority over the power of the enemy.

Now I might add that some of these things may seem a little radical, but they are the Word of God and not that of my own words. Preaching and teaching this might also get them kicked out of some churches, but I say again, it is the Word of God that is written in the Bible and can easily be read for themselves if they are in need of confirmation.

This is not about Religion or the do's and do not's or the you should do this or do that. This is about believing the Word of God and about His Grace, His Promises, His Mercy, His Faithfulness, His Love, and His Will for our lives.

He wants to have a true relationship and fellowship with us. He wants us to be a part of His Family.

There are some very important points I would like for you to remember as you are reading this book. I believe these points will help you to have a better and clearer understanding of what is being said.

First

Before the Cross of Jesus, we were under a period called the Law of God that Moses received from God on the mountain, but after the Cross Of Jesus, we are under a period called Grace. This makes a lot of difference in our relationship with God.

Second

God does not change, He is the same yesterday, today, and forever. God is no respector of persons, He loves us all and He does not want any of us to die in sin and be eternally seperated from Him.

He loved us so much that He made that salvation available to us through His Son Jesus, and by His gift of Grace to us.

Third

There is a big difference between Religion and a true born again Christian. Religion is the result of Jesus being crucified on the Cross. Religion did not acknowledge who Jesus was and is. The leaders of the religious groups and their legalism and self righteousness did not see Jesus as who He was and is today, The Son Of God. That Religion still exists today with it's modern day teaching of legalism and it's teaching of self righteousness. The do's and do not's. The if you want God to do something for you that you must do something for God first. This is not true, when Jesus died on the Cross it changed all that. It changed because of the Blood of Jesus redeeming us from the curse of the Law. It changed because we are no longer under the covenant of the Law but under a new covenant, the covenant of Grace. We have received our righteousness, our right standing with God because of what Jesus did on the Cross and has nothing to do with our self righteousness.

Fourth

Our true righteousness comes by what Jesus did and us believing in Him and what He did for us. When we come to Him and repent and confess to Him we need a Saviour and believe that He is the Saviour, with our mouth we confess unto salvation and when we believe that God raised Him from the dead we believe in our hearts unto righteousness. (Romans 10: 9-10)

You will be born again in your spirit and you will be sealed with God's Spirit, the Holy Spirit (Ephesians 1: 11-14) and (2 Corinthians 1:22) and not only that but you will become a child of God and receive the gift of eternal life.

Your spirit will never die. Your body will die. But you will never have to appear before The Great White Throne Judgement (2 Corinthians 5: 1-10) but will appear before The Judgement Seat Of Christ as a saved and redeemed by the Lord.

This is an all together different judgement than The Great White Throne Judgement Of God. The Judgement Seat Of Christ is the judgement of the saved and redeemed of the Lord. Those who received Jesus as their Saviour and Lord. There will be awards given or lost according to our works we have done with the abilites He has given us.

The works is not referring to our righteousness because you have been made righteous because of Jesus. You have became "The Righteous Of God In Christ" due to what Jesus has done and has nothing to do with us except by us believing in Him and accepting our salvation and the gift of Grace from God. (2 Corinthians 5:21). Jesus has done all He needed to do, He completed it all on the Cross, and that can not be changed. For He said on the Cross "It is Finished" and then He bowed His head and gave up His spirit to God. (John 19: 28-30)

Now understand that I am by no means saying that it is alright to sin, I am not. If you are truly a born again believer, the desire to sin willfully should not be present in your thoughts, and if you still desire to sin, Satan has a stronghold in your life and you need to ask God to help you break this stronghold and ask for forgiveness. What it is I am saying is that when we slip up and make a mistake and sin, We confess it to God and He is faithful and just to forgive us and purify us from unrighteousness, put us in right standing again with Him. (1 John 1:9)

When we receive spiritual gifts from God, we are expected to use them to bring glory to Him. Everyone has some kind of gift that God has blessed them with and we need to make every effort to learn what that gift is. Ask God to reveal that gift to you if you are having trouble knowing what it is but don't get stressed out trying to figure out what it is because God does not want you to get stressed out. He wants you to have peace in your life. Let Him help you and be patient and Rest in the Lord.

We all have a calling to lead people to the Lord and you can be sure of that. We are His voice in this world and He wants us to witness for Him. He puts people in our paths and orchestrates things from heaven for our blessings and for us to bless others. We are expected to bless others as we receive our blessing from Him.

There are rewards given for faithfulness and a loss of rewards for unfaithfulness. There are rewards given for our good works that He has graciously supplied us the means by which we may serve Him.

Our decision to serve and our determination to do so is left up to us to do it or not to do it. Our contribution to these things God will see and to Him these things are rewardable. He works in us both to will and to do as we appropriate His Grace to be a blessing to others. (Phillipians 2: 12-13).

This is not to say that you can repay God for our salvation, because that is a gift from God through Grace by faith, also another gift. You have not been saved through your works. (Ephesians 2: 8-9).

Paul said in (1 Corinthians 15:10) "But by the grace of God I am what I am, and His grace toward me did not prove vain, but I labored even more that all of them, yet not I, but the grace of God with me.")

In short, this judgement is a reward seat where rewards or the loss of rewards are judged. It is not a time of punishment where believers are judged for their sins, for their sins have been forgiven. If it were that type of judgement, it would put the finished work of Jesus on the Cross to no effect.

This is also to say that you should not wear yourself out trying to do good and in hopes that God will love you more or to make yourself more pleasing to God. He already loves you and you can do nothing to make Him love you more and that brings us to our next point, Resting In The Lord.

Fifth

Resting in the Lord involves several things. It may take some time to develop this Rest after you have been saved and become born again, but it will come.

You have to study the Word of God and get more understanding of who God is and His Will, His Promises, His Love and Care for us, and to truly trust and believe Him.

As you develop your fellowship with God and you begin to see Him working in your life, you will begin to trust Him and His Word more and more. You will come to the revelation that the more you trust Him and lean on His help that He is faithful to do the things He promised.

It takes faith, trust, understanding, and determination to stand in your faith in God to enter into His Rest.

It is God's will for our lives to be enjoyed by us. He wants us to have an abundant life full of joy, peace, love, health, prosperity, and worry free. Jesus bore all these things on the Cross for us so that we would not have to have them in our lives. It says in His Word that Satan tries to steal all these things from us. (John 10:10) "The thief comes to steal, kill, and destroy, but I have come to give you life and that life more abundantly."

When you truly enter into God's Rest, this life, this abundant life Jesus spoke of, is made available to us through God's Grace.

Remember God's Promises and remember God can not and will not lie. He will do what He said He would do.

God is Love and God is Holy, He is absolutely Holy with infinite uncomprehensible fullness of purity and He is incapable of being other that that. When God speaks, He will not and cannot lie, He never deceives or misrepresents what He says or does.

This means that God's Word, The Bible, is completely trustworthy and that the promises He has made to us will be carried out and done by Him.

These promises are still in effect today and will be throughout eternity because Jesus, the Christ, is the Fulfiller of the promises. (2 Corinthians 1: 20) "For all the promises of God find their yes in Him, That is why it is through Him that we utter our Amen to God for His Glory." In short, all God's promises are in Him is yes, and in Him Amen.

His promises are still fulfilled today through Christ, and we claim and receive them and acknowledge them by saying, Amen, which means, so be it.

That is why we must study the Word of God and learn what God's Will and promises are to us, and then pray to God for Him to answer that prayer with His promise that He has already made, and receive it by faith through God's Grace in the Name Of Jesus.

Knowing God Will and His Promises are important because you need to know them for your prayers to line up with His Word and be in accordance to His Will and His Promises in order for Him to answer your prayer.

Having faith in God is necessary and an absolute requirement needed for God to do anything at all for us. You cannot please God without faith (Hebrews 11: 6) "But without faith it is impossible to please God, for he who comes to God must believe that He is, and that He is a rewarder of those who earnestly seek Him."

When we got saved, we believed in God, Jesus, and the Holy Spirit. When we came to Him in our prayer for salvation we all received His free gift of Grace and we each received the same measure of faith. That faith grows as we learn and study the Word of God. (Romans 10: 17) "So then faith comes by hearing, and hearing by the word of God." The more faith you have and the more understanding of God's Word you have, the easier it is for you to trust God and to be able to enter into His Rest.

You will begin to not worry or to be anxious about things, you will begin to give your problems to God and trust Him to work them out. You will begin to focus on the promise instead of the problem, you will learn to not go by your feelings but by your faith, and you will learn that there truly is power in prayer.

Jesus told us this in (Mark 11: 24) "Therefore I say to you, whatsoever things you ask when you pray, believe that you receive them, and you will have them."

When you know the Will of God and your prayers are according to His Will and His Word, you will have what you ask if you ask in true faith and expect to receive what you ask.

The motives of your prayers are important. There are many different types of prayers, but all your prayers must line up to God's Will. If the motive of your prayers are of a selfish or lustful, that prayer won't be answered. In the Book of James, He says, (James 4:3) "You ask, and receive not, because you ask amiss, so that you may consume it upon your lusts."

It is God's Will to give us blessings and answers to our prayers, but it is not His Will for us to be selfish or lustful, and that type prayer will not be answered.

As mentioned before there are many different types of prayers and we will talk about them later in chapter 5. All prayers are important no matter how trivial some of them may seem. If it is important to you, it is important to God because He loves and cares for you.

God cares about you and does not want you to worry about things, He tells us to give Him our problem. (1 Peter 5:7) "To cast your cares upon Him, for He cares for you."

When you begin to fully rely on and trust God for all things, you have entered His Rest and you will have peace, true honest peace in your life. You will not be moved by the troubles going on around you for all your worry, anxiety, burdens, and cares have been passed on to God.

And here's why, God is at work in your life even when you don't realize it or understand it and it is more profitable to you when you cooperate with Him and let Him do what He said He would do. And you will see His Faithfulness to you in your life.

You begin to realize that there is a supernatural strength available to you from above and your perspective of life will change.

It is just as a loving caring earthly father, who truly cares for his children, does all he can do to be certain that all of his childrens needs are met, so it is with our Heavenly Father, but on a lot greater and grander scale, for He is The Almighty.

He is The Almighty God, Creator of Heaven and Earth, No one or anything is more powerful or more able than He is, and He is our Father. And that brings us to our next point, your Identity in God's Family.

Sixth

This is not referring to what denomination of church you go to or neither is it referring to what job or office you may hold in the church, it is referring to who you are as an individual to God and His Family.

When you got saved and born again, God sealed you with His Holy Spirit and you have His Spirit living inside you. That is when you became a child of God and He became your Father in Heaven.

When you are sealed with His Holy Spirit, that is like a down payment to you for your eternal life in Heaven with Him because you believe in Him and have received His Son Jesus as your Lord and Saviour. He is now living inside of you and your spirit and His Spirit bears witness with each other that you are a child of God.

Paul tells us about God's Holy Spirit living in us in (1 Corinthians 6: 19-20) "Do you not know that your bodies are temples of the Holy Spirit, who is in you, whom you received from God? You are not your own, you were bought at a price. Therefore honor God with your bodies." Jesus paid an incredible price for us, He gave His life.

If we are saved and have peace with God, and are led by His Spirit, we have nothing to fear in life or in death, our physical body death, because our eternity is secure as adopted sons and daughters of God. (Romans 8: 14-15) "For all who are led by the Spirit Of God are sons of God. For you did not receive the Spirit of fear, but you have received the Spirit Of Adoption as sons by whom we cry Abba Father."

The word Abba is an Aramic word that would most closely be defined as the word Daddy. How awesome is that. The scripture says sons of God but this also means daughters of God as well.

Now some people who are not saved but believe only in the existence of God would say that we are all the children of God, but that is not true. We are all His creation and will be judged by Him, but being a child of God and having the right to truly call Him Abba Father, or Daddy, is something that only born again Christian believers are entitled to do.(John 1: 12-13) "But to all who did receive

Him, (Jesus) who believed in His name, (Jesus) He gave the right to become children of God, who were born, not of the blood nor of the will of the flesh nor of the will of man, but of God." Now that is pretty plain, if they have not received Jesus and believed in Him, then they are not a child of God.

So when you became a child of God when you got saved and born again, you also became an heir to God and a co-heir with Jesus (Romans 8: 16-17) "The Spirit Himself bears witness with our spirit that we are children of God. And if children, then heirs of God and joint heirs with Christ. If indeed we suffer with Him, that we may be glorified together." He has promised us an eternal inheritance and it is based on the worthiness of Christ Himself.

This suffering it speaks of is the persecution that we receive in this world because of our faith and belief and our constant battle within ourselves by trying to mortify the deeds of our flesh and get it under the control of the Spirit and glorifying God.

This worthiness of our promise of having an eternal inheritance is based on the worthiness of Christ Himself, not ours. God tells us how we have been brought near to Him by the Blood Of Jesus. (Ephesians 2: 13) "In Christ Jesus you who were once far away have been brought near by the blood of Christ."

We became adopted children by God, we became a brother to Jesus our Lord, brothers and sisters to other believers, and the church became our spiritual family. As believers we all became children of God through faith in Christ Jesus. (Galatians 3: 26) "You are all children of God through faith in Christ Jesus."

When God sees us as a born again believer, He sees us through the Blood Of Jesus. He sees our righteousness through the Righteousness Of Jesus because of His shed blood for us. We have been made the Righteousness Of God In Christ and not of ourselves but because of Jesus.(2 Corinthians 5:21) "God made Him who had no sin to be sin for us, so that in Him we might become the Righteousness Of God."

We need to remember this when Satan comes to condemn us for something we did in the past, or for that matter, any sin, past, present, or future because God told us in His Word that when we mess up and sin and confess it to Him that He would forgive us and bring us back into right standing with Him.(1 John 1:9) "If we confess our sin, He is faithful and just to forgive us our sin and cleanse us from all unrighteousness."

When we confess it, God forgives it, and we are back in right standing with God again. So Satan has no right to condemn you and you need to use your authority over Satan and He will flee from you. You have authority over Satan and we will talk about that in chapter 5.

Remember your identity in God's Family. You are a child of God. You are an heir to God and a co-heir with Christ. Jesus is your older brother and your Lord, You have the spiritual DNA of Jesus, and you have been adopted into God's Family.

How great is that, being a son or daughter of The Most High God, Almighty God, The Creator Of All Things, and being a younger brother or sister to The Lord Of Lords and The King of Kings. Think about it. That is who you are in Christ.

Always remember what you mean to God and your indentity in His Family. He loves us so much that He sacraficed His beloved Son, Jesus, to save us from an eternal damnation and to give us an abundant life meant to be full of joy, peace, and love. His love is unconditional and is from everlasting to everlasting.

He loves us so much that He sent His Spirit to live in us and guide us, strengthen us, and educate us in His Word and in His Ways. He protects us when we are in need of protection. He gives us peace and not fear. He blesses us and supplies our needs.

He has made promises that He will keep if we will do our part of the covenant that He has made with us and our father Abraham for we are the seed of Abraham. (Galatians 3: 26-29) "For ye are all the children of God by faith in Christ Jesus. For as many of you as have been baptized into Christ have put on Christ. There is neither Jew nor Greek, bond or free, or male or female: for you all are one in Christ Jesus. And if you be Christ's, then are you the seed of Abraham, and heir according to the promise."

We are protected and watched over by our most powerful and everlasting Father in Heaven. (Psalm 91: 1-2) "Whoever dwells in the shelter of the Most High will rest in the shadow of the Almighty, and I will say of the Lord, He is my refuge and my fortress, my God, in whom I will trust." You could say it this way, whoever dwells in the shelter of Our Father in Heaven will not have to worry about being protected because He is our shelter and protector, and in Him I will trust.

That is an awesome protection, and if we will do our part and trust and obey what He says, we will be under that great protection. Read Psalm 91 and get the full meaning of it.

Now I am going to make a statement about Psalm 91 and it may seem to be a little radical to some people, but read it for yourself. There are 3 voices speaking in this Psalm. In verses 1 and 2, as we just stated, it is David and also us speaking, in verses 3 through 13, it is Jesus speaking, and in verses 14 through 16, it is God speaking. Read it for yourself and keep this in mind when you read it and you will see it is true.

Now you may ask how could this be Jesus since this was before the time of Jesus and His Ministry here on earth. Well let's talk about that for a few minutes.

Jesus was in the beginning with God in Heaven before coming to earth by the incarnate birth when the Holy Spirit overshadowed the Virgin Mary and Jesus was born and grew up as a man here on earth. Jesus was in the beginning with God at creation, He was and is "The Word of God" and all things were made through Him and without Him nothing was made and The Word was made flesh and dwelt among us. (John 1: 1-14).

From Genesis to Malachi in the Old Testament, it foretells that Christ would come into the world. This is why Jesus tells the Jewish leaders during His time here on earth about (John 5: 39) "You study the scriptures earnestly because you think that in them you have eternal life. These are the very scriptures that testify of me."

In many places in the Old Testament it talks about Angels. There are "Angels of the Lord" or "An Angel of the Lord" and "The Angel of the Lord." In speaking of "The Angel of the Lord" it has a unique being, seperate from the other Angels. "The Angel of the Lord" speaks as God. Many scriptures refer to "The Angel of the Lord (Genesis 16: 7-12)(Genesis 21: 17-18)(Genesis 22: 11-13) (Exodus 3: 2) and several other places in Judges, Samuel, and Zechariah.

It is clear in some of these instances that "The Angel of the Lord" appeared as God in physical form, and remember that Jesus is God the Son.

The appearance of "The Angel of the Lord" ceased after the incarnation of Jesus and His birth. The appearence of Angels in the New Testament refer to "a Angel or Angels of the Lord" or "An Angel of the Lord" and because Jesus was "The Angel of the Lord" and His appearance ceased when Jesus became flesh here on earth. And now after His resurrection and going to be with His Father He had the Father send His Holy Spirit to live in us.

My purpose in even mentioning this is to give an idea of how close a family we are to God. Before Jesus was crucified and raised from the dead and before we received His Holy Spirit, God sent "The Angel of the Lord" to communicate with His people. But now because we have been saved and born again and have become children of God and have His Holy Spirit living in us and we are one in Him and He is one in us, we can communicate directly with God through and by His Holy Spirit.

How awesome is that, we can talk to Him just as we can talk to one another.

Just as Jesus is one in the Father and the Father is one in Him, we are one in Jesus. We are one in Christ and have been sanctified (set apart) from the unbelievers and joined together with Jesus.

Jesus prayed this to His Father and our Father in John 17. He was not only praying for His disciples but also for us and for anyone who believes in Him and what He has done. (John 17: 16-23) "They are not of the world, even as I am not of the world. Sanctify them through thy truth: thy word is truth. As thou has sent me into the world, even so have I also sent them into the world. And for their sakes I sanctify myself, that they also might be sanctified through the truth. I do not pray for these alone, but for them also which shall believe on me through their word. That they all may be one, as thou, Father, art in me, and I in thee, that they also may be one in us: that the world may believe that thou has sent me. And the glory which thou gavest me I have given them, that they may be one, even as we are one: I in them, and thou in me, that they may be perfect in one; and that the world may know that thou has sent me, and has loved me, and has loved them, as thou has loved me." This is a close family. Don't ever forget how much God loves us and how close we are to Him and His Son, our Lord and Saviour, Jesus, and His Holy Spirit.

He is always with us and never leaves us or abandons us, He has always got time to hear us when we pray, He watches over us and knows our needs, and He wants us to ask Him for help when we need it. He is our Father, He loves us and cares for us.

He wants to be a part of our lives all the time because He is a loving, caring, and merciful God who desires to have fellowship with us as His children and as our Father.

Now I have mentioned all of this for the purpose of giving you an idea of who God truly is to us and who we are to Him.

These are only a few things about God, our Father, that we need to keep in mind as we continue in this book. There are so many other benefits of being a born again believer and we will mention them later. I believe they will be a real blessing to you and will make the quality of your life so much better.

Remembering all these things that you have already read and putting them into practice in your everyday life will not only bless you and give you a more abundant and happy life, but will also bring peace that surpasses all earthly understanding. And not only that, but it will give you the assurance and hope that God truly loves us and cares for us in this life and our eternal life to come.

Before we go any further in this book, we need to know if we are born again, and if we are saved. If you are not sure, or if you have never received Jesus as your Lord and Saviour and you have that desire to do so, then pray the prayer that is on the following page and mean it with all your heart and He will hear you. For all the things I have mentioned before about our relationship and fellowship with God are only avaiable to you if you are a born again believer.

If and when you pray this prayer, mean it with all your heart and all your mind. Also believe it with all that is in you and do not doubt that He will hear you because He will.

This is a prayer that He has always wanted you to pray and He will be very happy to answer it if you are truly sincere.

He does not want anyone to be lost and seperated from Him. He does not want for anyone to suffer in eternal torment. He does not want anyone to go through those things you read about in chapter 1. He did not create Hell for us but for Satan and his fallen angels that followed him out of heaven. God never intended for mankind to go to Hell but to have fellowship with Him here on earth and in Heaven.

When you pray this prayer, speak it out loud. say it with your mouth, not because God cannot hear you if you say it silently, but where Satan can hear you denounce him and he will realize that he has no more control over you because you have now become a child of God and re-gained that authority over him because of the Blood of Jesus and the authority that Jesus gave us over the devil and all his evil.

Satan will still come and try to control you and that is why you need to know the Word of God. He has no right to do it legally and until you know this and know what to do to fight him off, he will continue to try.

That is why I have written this book, to help you know how and what to do when he tries to overtake you.

Please say the following prayer with all your heart and do not doubt, only believe.

<u>Say this Out Loud</u> Because confession is made with the mouth.

"Dear Jesus, I come to you today realizing that I need a Saviour, and I know that you are The Saviour. I know that I have not received you as my Lord and my Saviour. I ask you now to be my Lord and Saviour and to forgive me for all of my sins, and I forgive anyone who has ever sinned against me. I believe that you are the Son of God and was crucified on the Cross and took my sins upon yourself so that I could be reconciled to the Father in Heaven. I believe that you died and God raised you from the dead and that you are seated at the Right Hand of God in Heaven. Come live in me and help me to become the person you want me to be. I receive you as my Lord and Saviour and thank you for what you have done for me and I thank you for hearing my prayer. Amen"

If you prayed this prayer and truly meant it with all your heart and did not doubt in your heart that God heard you, you have been saved and have been born again. Yes it is that simple, if you truly meant the prayer.

You have been sealed with God's Holy Spirit. You have become the Righteousness Of God In Christ because you have believed in Jesus and what He has done and you have confessed it with your words.

Find a good church that teaches the true Word of God and start reading the Bible and begin to study the Word of God and ask His Holy Spirit to help you understand as you study His Word.

And here is a good scripture to begin with from the Word of God just in case you may have even the slightest doubt of you being saved and born again. There should be no doubt. (Romans 10: 9-10) "If you shall confess with your mouth the Lord Jesus, and shall believe in your heart that God has raised Him from the dead, you shall be saved. For with the heart man believeth unto righteousness, and with the mouth confession is made unto salvation." That is what you just did and if you truly believe it and meant it, you are saved and born again.

If you are one who just did this, welcome to the Family of God, for the Angels in Heaven are rejoicing right now in the Presence of God on your behalf. Glory Be To God and Praise His Holy Name. Hallelujah !!!

Remember all the things I have mentioned previously in this book. Read and study the Word of God and get it deep down into your spirit and believe it with all your heart, and with all your mind. Stand in your faith and let not anyone or anything alter that faith or compromise the Word of God.

Your spirit is brand new but your body and soul, which is your mind, will, and emotions will need to make some adjustments so that you will begin to think as God wants you to think and to be conformed to God's System of doing things instead of the world's system. (Romans 12: 1-2) I urge you therefore, brothers and sisters, by the mercies of God, that you present your bodies as a living sacrifice, holy, and acceptable unto God, which is your reasonable service. And be not conformed to this world, but be ye transformed by the renewing of your mind, that you may prove what is that good and acceptable, and perfect will of God."

A good motivation to live for Christ is a good memory of all His mercies that He has blessed us with, and His promise that He will always be with us and never leave us or abandon us.

In the scripture just mentioned, Paul said to present our bodies as a living sacrifice and that is our spiritual act of worship to God. To present our bodies as to be holy and acceptable to God is to be wholly dedicated and "set apart" from the world and for us to belong to God and to discipline ourselves to be as pleasing to God as much as we can. We are to acknowledge Him in all that we do and we should worship Him in truth and in spirit. Worship should become a lifestyle and not just a Sunday thing. Resolve to make worship a priority in your life, talk to God everyday, and let Him know that you want Him to be a big part of your life.

This all comes from changed minds, transforming your mind, because the mind will control your actions and your thoughts. The world has its own way of thinking, its philosophy, its understanding and opinions, but God's Word and God's Ways are a lot different from that of the world. The world has its system and God has His System.

So he says do not be conformed to the world, but transform your mind to think on God's System and His way of doing things. Read, absorb, and interact with God's Word. Have faith in His Word and do not have faith in the things in this world. For the world will fail you if you put your trust in it and not in God.

The world can be selfish, self-centered, unloving, uncaring. But God is love, God is caring, God wants to bless us. So set your mind on these things and please God, and prove His perfect will, show His goodness, show His mercy, and love and kindness to others. These things do, and show the love of God to others and be like Christ. For that is what a Christian is, to be "Christ-like."

Seventh

Put your trust in God. Do not put your trust in the world as I mentioned before. As you read and study the Word of God and meditate on on His Word, you will grow in your faith, and your understanding. For the Word says, (Romans 10: 17) "So then faith comes by hearing, and hearing by the Word of God." When troubles come in life, and they will, for the Word says they will, put your trust and faith in God and don't try to understand everything on your own. Rather trust and let God work things out for you and turn your burdens over to Him.(Proverbs 3: 5-6) "Trust in the Lord with all your heart and lean not to your own understanding, in all your ways, acknowledge Him, and He will direct your paths." He will give you guidance. (Psalm 55: 22) "Give your burdens to the Lord and He will take care of you, He will not permit the righteous to be shaken." He truly cares for us and He will help us in our time of need if we will truly believe and put our trust in Him and not doubt.

He is always with us, shields us, and protects us. (Psalm 16: 8) "I know the Lord is always with me. I will not be shaken, for He is right beside me." He protects us Himself (Psalm 121:5) "The Lord Himself watches over you. The Lord stands beside you as your protective shade."

If you should begin to worry about things, give the problem to the Lord and He will help you. Jesus said, (Matthew 11:28) "Come to me, all who labor and are heavy laden, and I will give you rest."

These scriptures should give the idea that God will do the things I have been talking about. Now there is sometimes things that do happen that God will allow us to go through, notice I said go through, because you will make it through it and always remember that God is right there with you. And these things happen to build character in us and strengthen us and build our faith. God knows what is the best for us even if we don't understand it at the time, but I say it again, "Trust in the Lord and lean not to your own understanding."

In order for us to truly please God, we need to trust Him and have faith in Him and His Word.

If we never give God the opportunity to help us, then we are not giving Him the opportunity to show His Faithfulness to us and we are not showing our faith in Him.

God gives us a free will, He does not force Himself on anyone. It is up to us and our choice and our will to decide whether to work with or against God. But it is to our advantage to work with Him and not against Him and that is another reason why it is important to know and understand the Word of God.

Now there are sometimes other reasons that things happen in our lives that God does not want to happen and He wants to help us but He is limited on what He can do. We will talk about these things in chapter 5 regarding our God given Authority.

I know I have said a lot in this chapter, but it is for the reason of trying to get the points across about the love and character of God, who we are to God, who He is to us, and the relationship and fellowship He wants to have with us.

There are still a lot of things that need to be said about our relationship and our fellowship with God and it is my intention to identify some of these things in the following chapters.

Now I might add that some of the information in some of these following chapters may be a little radical and is not a welcome subject in some churches, However, it needs to be said no matter how controversial they may be, and it is the Word of God, and God wants us to know these things.

These things that we will talk about in chapter 5, 6, and 7, can actually change our lives and make a huge difference in the quality of our lives and our victory over Satan and his activities and deception. I know that it has in my life and it can make a difference in yours as well.

Now if you prayed the Prayer Of Salvation that is in this chapter, and have become a brand new believer, let us talk about the baptism of water and the baptism of the Holy Spirit and your Kingdom Rights first before we get into the rest. It is important because you have became a child of God and a citizen of His Kingdom.

CHAPTER 3

BAPTISM OF WATER AND
BAPTISM OF THE HOLY SPIRIT

There are many different beliefs and teaching on water baptism in churches, and the doctrines, requirements, and administering the baptism differ as well.

Many questions have evolved from these differences. Questions like: Do I get baptized by full immersion, sprinkling, or the pouring the water over me? Do I have to be baptized to be saved? What is the purpose of baptism?

All this questions are important and can cause confusion to many. It may even cause a stumbling block to some people in their faith.

So let's look at what the Word of God says about the matter.

First of all, the purpose of being baptized is symbolic and used as a public profession of your faith and your dedication in serving God. When you are immersed in under the water you are symbolizing that your old self, your sinful nature, is put to death and relates to the death of Christ on the Cross. When you come out of the water, it symbolizes that you are a new creature, that you are raised from being dead to sin and death and made alive in Christ and have resurrected into eternal life, relating to the Resurrection Of Jesus.

Perhaps an easier way of saying this is, being submerged under water represents death to sin, and emerging from the water represents the cleansed holy life that follows salvation. (Romans 6: 4) "We were buried therefore with Him by baptism into death, in order that, just as Christ was raised from the dead by the glory of the Father, that we too might walk in the newness of life." Also Paul tells us in 2nd chapter of the book of Colossians (Colossians 2: 12) "Buried with Him in baptism, wherein also you are risen with Him through faith of the operation of God, who raised Him from the dead."

A baptism does not save you. The finished work of Jesus on the Cross and His Blood shed for us and our believing in Him is what saves us. We are saved by the Grace of God through faith in Jesus and what He has done. (Ephesians 2: 8-9) "For by grace are you saved through faith, and that not of yourselves: it is a gift of God, and not of works, lest any man should boast." We do not have to do anything or add anything to the finished work of Jesus on the Cross, if we did, we would be saying the Cross was not enough.

However, as a born again believer, we should desire to be baptized as a public profession of our faith and discipleship. It says in effect that we confess our faith in Christ and that Jesus took away our sins and cleansed us from all unrighteousness and that we now have a new life in Christ.

It also, to me personally, says to God our Father and our Lord Jesus that I do this in honor and gratitude of what you have done for me. I show my humility and my respect and my reverence to you, I do this as an action of showing my dedication and my desire to serve you. Now that is just my personal feelings and not a requirement.

A baptism dramatizes the death, burial, and resurrection of Jesus, And it illustrates death to sin and a new life in Christ. It does not keep you from going to heaven.

In (Luke 23: 39-43) the thief on the cross did not have the opportunity to get baptized, but he believed in who Jesus truly was, and on that same day, he went to Paradise with Jesus.

Jesus did command us to preach the Gospel and to baptize them who got saved, He told us this in (Matthew 28: 18-19) "And Jesus came and spoke to them, saying, All power is given to me in heaven and in earth. Go ye therefore, and teach to all of the nations, baptizing them in the name of the Father, and of the Son, and of the Holy Ghost."

Jesus Himself was baptized by John the Baptist eventhough He nad no sin, but He told John to do it so that all Righteousness would be fulfilled.(Matthew 3: 13-15) It seems that in order for all things to be fulfilled for Jesus to complete His work, that is was necessary for Him to be baptized by John.

Now remember that this was all before the Cross and Jesus was still under the period of the Law of the Torah, the writing of Moses, and everyone was supposed to be under the Priests of the Old Testament.

The baptism that John was doing had the function of purifying as the Torah taught about people being unclean and they needed to be purified in order to be restored to their status in the community, but John's preaching about Repentance and for the forgiveness of sins along with it fulfilled the Old Testament prophecy in preparing the way for the Messiah that was spoken of in (Isaiah 40)

Now is baptism necessary? I would say yes, and it is not because it saves you, but because it is an act of obedience to the command of Jesus in Matthew 28 that we need to do it.

Is it important to be baptized to fulfill all Righteousness as it was with Jesus? All Righteousness was fulfilled by Jesus for us when He went to the Cross. When we received Him as our Saviour and

Lord and the Holy Spirit came to live in us, we became The Righteousness Of God In Christ.(2 Corinthians 5: 21) "For He (God) has made Him (Jesus) who knew no sin, to be sin for us, that we might be made the Righteousness Of God in Him (Christ)."

Jesus was obeying His Father and so it should be with us. So if it be for no other reason that someone may think of baptism being important, we should do it because Jesus commanded it.

Now the question, should I be submerged, sprinkled, or poured over? Well in the Old Testament it was by submerging under the water. The Greek word baptizo means to dip. The Hebrew word tevilah means to dip. The Greek word baptizen means to immerse, and in English it refers to convert or recruit.

The Roman Catholic Church used immersion until 1311 AD then it changed to sprinkling. The Lutheran Church teach that a valid baptism must include the use of water along with using the Word. Martin Luther consistently taught that only water and the Word constitute one baptism. It was not the way the water was applied.

The New Testament contains no explicit instruction on how to administer a water baptism, but it seems to lean more in the direction of submersion than to sprinkling or pouring.

So we can see that there are several different beliefs about baptism. However, I feel that the mode used is not as important as the purpose of it. The use of water is for the purpose of symbolic cleansing. The emphasis should be on idenifying the one being baptized with a cleansing provided by God Himself, and the person publicly professing their faith and their conversion.

So without a firm foundation of the Word in the New Testament and no explicit instruction written it it, I can not say which way is right or wrong. Most churches dictate their mode of baptism in accordance to their denomination and it's through this baptism that a person is admitted to the church as a menber.

When you choose a church to start your fellowship with other believers, pray to the Father that His Holy Spirit will guide you to the right church. Keep in mind that not all churches believe alike. It is from my own experience, if a church does not believe in the Baptism of The Holy Spirit and is not subject to allow the freedom of The Holy Spirit to move freely during the church service and among the fellowship of all the believers, I will not become a part of that church.

Now this is not to say that those type of churches are not true believers or that they are bad people, I am saying that if we as a child of God and a royal citizen to His Kingdom are to achieve victory in our lives over Satan and all his deceptions and afflictions and we are to live that abundant life that Jesus spoke of, then we have to allow the Holy Spirit to work freely in our lives.

We are not to quench the Holy Spirit, some churches have the attitude of contempt towards God's supernatural gifting of believers. Some believers neglect the gift that they may have by not using it and that quenches the Spirit. Some neglect the word of prophesy that was spoken to them by the elders laying hands on them and that quences the Spirit. This is not to say we have power over the Spirit of God, for we do not, it is to say that we sometimes do not give His Holy Spirit the freedom to work in our lives as He desires to do.

Some churches do an excellent job of preaching salvation and bringing people to Jesus, and this is very important because it is the number 1 thing and it is what God wants us to do. It is the most important decision that a person can make because it can determine where they will spend eternity.

But it does not have to end there and it does with some churches. It is written that we can have an abundant life by God changing things in our lives right here and right now while we are still here on earth. We do not have to wait until we get to Heaven. But in order for these things to happen, we must cooperate with God and His Holy Spirit.

We must realize that all of these things in life, our salvation, our righteousness, our healing, our peace, our deliverance, our prosperity, our identity in God's Family, our God given authority, and all things pertaining to our abundant life, has already been provided and made available to us by The Blood Of Jesus and by the Grace of God.

I have mentioned all of this for the purpose of showing how important it is for us to be Baptized with the Holy Spirit in order to receive the wisdom and the power from God to do His Will here on earth. And be sure you know this, without Him, we can do nothing.

Some churches do not believe in this and other churches believe that being Baptized with the Holy Spirit takes place when you get saved. Well let us see what the Word of God says about this.

First of all, we need to know that the Holy Spirit is one Spirit, that He is a He and not a it. He is very much a Divine part of God's Trinity and when we get saved and refer to being born again, we all receive the same Spirit. (1 Corinthians 12: 12-13) "For as the body is one, and has many members, and all the members of that one body, being many, are one body, so also is Christ. For by one Spirit are we all baptized into one body, whether we be Jews or Gentiles, bond or free; and have been all made to drink into one Spirit."

Now this scripture is talking about spiritual gifts and the different operations in different believers and how the same Spirit works in them to perform these different operations. This also is the same Spirit that God seals believers with when we get saved. (Ephesians 1: 13-15) "In who you also trusted, after that you have heard the word of truth, the gospel of your salvation, in whom also after that you believed, you were sealed with the Holy Spirit of Promise, which is the earnest of our inheritance until the redemption of the purchased possession, unto the praise of His glory."

Jesus' Blood has purchased our redemption. We are now His and the Fathers possession in this life and our eternal life with Him. He has put His seal, the Holy Spirit, on us and in us. It is His deposit or earnest in our hearts that He claims us as His very own, and has given us believers a down payment on our heavenly inheritance.

Now what I have just spoken about is God sealing us with His Holy Spirit when we get saved as I talked about earlier in chapter 2. Now this is not to be confusing or misunderstood as to being the same thing as a believer being baptized with the Holy Spirit. This is an after salvation experience and with the help of Paul's gospel, I will try to explain.

At one point in the Apostle Paul's life and Ministry, he was the pastor of a local congregation in an ancient city in Greece called Ephesus. While he was serving as the pastor, he came in contact with some of John the Baptist's former disciples. These disciples believed everything John preached about the coming of Jesus the Messiah but they had not yet heard the full Message of the Gospel. They had not heard about the need to be born again and making Jesus the Lord of their life. They knew nothing about the Baptism of the Holy Spirit which had come on the Day of Pentecost some weeks after Jesus ascended into Heaven. (Acts 2: 1-5)

The Apostle Paul explained to them how to make Jesus their Lord and Saviour, leading them into that experience. After they accepted Jesus and became members into the body of Christ and being born again, Paul told them of another experience after their salvation called the Baptism with Holy Spirit.

This is a special Baptism of Power still available today to all who are a born again believer. Paul led them into this experience as well. He laid his hands on them and they were baptized with the Holy Spirit and they all spoke with tongues and prophesied. It talks about this in (Acts 19: 1-6)

A lot of churches do not believe in the speaking with tongues or the laying of hands on someone who is sick and using that God given delegated authority given to us born again believers to cast out sickness or demons.

It makes no difference whether they believe it or not, it does not change the fact that it is a true God given gift that He does through His Holy Spirit in us and through us true born again believers to do His Will here on earth. It is a command of Jesus for us to do this. We will talk about this more in chapter 5 of this book.

The greatest gift God gave the world was His Son Jesus so that through Him they could receive their new birth in Jesus Christ, and the greatest gift God has ever given to His born again children is the Baptism of His Holy Spirit and the gift of Grace.

Now some people may call the Baptism of the Holy Spirit the same as the Filling of the Holy Spirit. All born again believers are equally saved and equally sealed with the Holy Spirit, but not all believers are equally filled with His Spirit. They have not fully yeilded or surrendered themselves to God and the leading of His Spirit.

The filling of the Holy Spirit is a part of sanctification, or setting us apart, from the non-believers and the worldly system. It is a part of our discipleship to Christ. But the filling of the Holy Spirit is not that we get more of Him but that He gets more of us. It is not a one time event, it is a continual process which is part of our growing spiritually.

Spiritual maturity is not measured by the time someone has been a believer, it is rather by their growth in knowledge, understanding, fellowship, and yielding more to the control of the Holy Spirit.

In chapter 5 of Ephesians, Paul is giving instruction in being followers of God. He talks about fleshy things and spiritual things and gives warnings about being seperated and have no fellowship with the works of darkness. He tells us to walk upright, not as a fool, but as of the wise. He tells us not to be unwise, but to understand what the Will of the Lord is. He also compares and tells us how being drunk with wine and being filled with the Spirit are opposite of each other but they both have a powerful influence in our lives. (Ephesians 5: 18) "And be not drunk with wine, wherein is excess, but be filled with the Spirit."

In chapter 4 of Ephesians, Paul is also giving instruction on how we are all one body in Christ and talks about the 5 Ministry gifts, our spiritual growth, and how we are to walk worthy of our calling.

There are different gifts of the Spirit, but it is the same Spirit that does them all, there are different Anointing on different people, but it is the same Spirit works through them all.

It is all by the Grace of God and His Holy Spirit leading and teaching us as born again believers that we can do anything to make our life the way God intended for it to be. God teaches and gives instruction to us through and by His Word and His Holy Spirit helps us to understand and guides us through the process.

We need His Holy Spirit to help us to do all things that will give us the ability to have victory in our lives. We need Him to teach us and help us understand the wisdom of God's Word, we need Him to help us to do God's Will and to lead others to Jesus, we need Him to produce the power needed when we use our God given authority against Satan, we need Him to help us to love one another, in short, we need Him for all things. We need the Baptism of the Holy Ghost.

CHAPTER 4

OUR KINGDOM RIGHTS AND RESPONSIBILITIES

When you are born again, you are born into the family of God. You have not only become a child of God. "A chosen people" you have also become a citizen of the Kingdom of God "a holy nation" which is a real kingdom with covenant rights for its citizens.

This kingdom is a Spiritual Kingdom, it has spiritual laws, and a kingdom form of government. As a follower of Christ we are expected to learn how to live here on earth that is consistent with our royal status in God's Kingdom and we are expected to learn God's Word, how these spiritual laws work, and to obey our King and His teachings.

The Bible says that those who make Jesus both their Saviour and Lord become citizens of God's Kingdom. So one would think that it would be wise to understand the kingdom, its culture, its laws, and its government. Why? Because in a kingdom your rewards are tied to being obedient to the king. And in the case of the Kingdom of God, they are tied to being obedient to The King. (John 8: 31-32) "If you hold to my teaching, you are really my disciples. Then you will know the truth, and the truth will set you free." Jesus also said (John 14: 23) "If anyone loves me, he will obey my teaching. My Father will love him, and we will come to him and make our home with him."

Most Americans don't understand the kingdom form of government and most churches are not teaching their people about the Kingdom of God and about the spiritual laws and how God's Word governs it, Christ wants them to do this.

The dictionary defines a kingdom "as a politically organized community or major territory having a monarchy type of government headed by a king or queen."

The Kingdom of God is under the control of a Righteous King, Our Saviour and our Lord Jesus, The Christ. He is the government, power, and authority of this kingdom.

A kingdom form of government is more superior than other forms because:

1. The primary focus of a righteous king is the well-being of the people under his authority.
2. Decisions are based on truth and what is right rather than what is politically or personally in the best interest of a person or party.
3. A citizen of a kingdom, is under the protection of the king and his kingdom.
4. You have freedom and rewards if you obey the king and comply with his culture.
5. The kingdom form of government is the natural order of things in the universe.

The following are some characteristics of a kingdom form of government.

1. A king is never voted into power, he is born into power.
2. A king cannot be voted out of power.
3. A king determines who will be its citizens and the standards for becoming a citizen.
4. In a righteous kingdom, the welfare of the citizens is the responsibilty of the king.
5. The word of the king is law and he is bound by it. His word cannot be changed, or challenged by anyone.
6. The authority of a king is unconditional. It can not be changed by anyone or any government body.
7. In a kingdom government, the king is the government. He doesn't represent the government, he is the government. He does not represent the authority, he is the authority. Where he goes the government and all its power and authority is present.
8. The kings authority is delegated through his name and he can delegate authority to act in his name or on his behalf.
9. In a kingdom the king owns everything, there is no personal ownership, only the stewardship over the kings property.
10. In a kingdom, the king has a realm and a reign. The realm is the territory and boundaries of which a king reigns and the reign is his rule, power, or authority.

I have put this information about the structure of a kingdom on these pages to help to try to show how the Kingdom of God works on this earth and in our lives.

The focus of Jesus' teaching on earth was twofold. He came to define reality, to execute a plan of restoration of mankind and His creation, to reconcile mankind to God and to reestablish the kingdom of God on earth.

God gave humans authority to rule the earth when He created them, but they lost that authority when they disobeyed God in the Garden Of Eden and that is when Satan stole it from man and assumed dominion over the earth.

Satan demonstrates that dominion **he had** when he was in the process of tempting Jesus in the wilderness. (Matthew 4: 8-9) "Again, the devil took him (Jesus) to a very high mountain and showed Him all the kingdoms of the world and their splendor. And the devil said to Jesus, all this I will give you if you will bow down and worship me"

But Thanks be to God, remember I said in chapter 1 that Jesus **took back** this power and authority from Satan when He went to Hades between His death and His Resurrection and stripped Satan of all his authority and took the keys to Hell, death, and the grave. That gave us as believers victory over death and Satan could not use that as a fear factor any longer for a born again believer. That was the number 4 on the characteristics of a kingdom list. The king takes responsibility for the welfare of His citizens.

And not only that, but as we will talk about in chapter 5 of this book, Jesus delegated that same authority He had over Satan and all of his evil to us as born again believers. Remember that was the number 8 on the characteristics of a kingdom list. The king can delegate His authority. Jesus delegated that authority to us in (Luke 10:19)

Something very powerful happens in the heart of a believer when they begin to understand what it means to be a kingdom citizen with kingdom rights. When we are confronted by Satan and his attacks and accusations, it is important for us to understand that we have rights, and to know how through faith to use these rights and authority that has been given to us.

But we have more than just rights in the kingdom. We are adopted children of God and a part of God's family, an heir to God Himself and a joint heir with Jesus.

We have kingdom rights and family rights to use against the devil when he comes to kill, steal, and destroy. We have the protection of Angels from our Father in Heaven, we have that delegated authority over Satan and all evil, we have the Power of God living inside of us, and God helps us to fight our battles. So as it is written (Romans 8:31) "If God be for us, who can be against us." There is no one who has more power, more authority, or more love and compassion than Almighty God, the creator of all things. He is our "Daddy" in Heaven, our forever present help in our time of need, and He has sent His Spirit to come live in us and help us. (1 John 4:4) "You are of God, little children, and have overcome them, because He who is in you is greater than he who is in the world."

A person may have heard these scriptures before, but if they did not realize it at the time about who they are, their indentity, their rights, their protection and all of the things mentioned before about who we are in Christ and they have now come to realize it, these scriptures should take on a whole new meaning to them. They should plainly see that God does not abandon us and that He is a ever present help in our time of need and that He is always with us and loves us very much.

He truly loves us and cares for us and will not leave us as orphans or abandon us when we need Him the most.

We have our rights as a citizen in the Kingdom of God and as a child of God. And in addition to these rights we also have responsibilities. Many believers today that know these rights are quick and eager to grab hold of them but are far less eager to grab hold of the responsibility that comes along with it. Jesus paid the ultimate sacrafice to make available the rights and priviledges that we have inherited from what He has already done, and now it is time for us to do our part as kingdom citizens.

We have the responsibility to show God's love and to help others because Jesus commanded us to do so. We have the responsibility to help those who may have a weaker or an undeveloped faith and have a lack of understanding of the Word of God. We need to help them to become stronger and have a better understanding. It is written in (Romans 15: 1-2) "Those of us who are strong and able in faith need to step in and lend a hand to those who falter, and not just do what is most convenient for us. Strength is for service, and not status. Each one of us needs to look after the good of the people around us, asking ourselves, How can I help?"

We all need to stay true to God's purpose in our lives. God loves us unconditionally and because God is love, He wants us to love and care for others. He wants us to show and demonstrate His love and how He cares for all of us.

If we are to be a true follower of Jesus, we must love one another. He commanded us to do so. (John 13: 34-35) "A new command I give you. Love one another. As I have loved you, so you must love one another. By this everyone will know that you are my disciples, if you love one another."

If we are to be a true follower of Jesus, we must help others if we have the means to do it. (1 John 3: 17) "But if anyone has the world's goods and he sees his brother in need, yet closes his heart against him, how does God's love abide in him."

When you help others, it does not go unnoticed by God. It is written in the Book of Proverbs (Proverbs 19:17) "Whoever is generous to the poor lends to the Lord, and He will repay him for his deed." Now this is not to say to do something expecting something in return, that is the wrong motive, do it out of kindness and love, it is then God will be pleased and will notice. It is also written in the Book of Proverbs (Proverbs 28:27) "Whoever gives to the poor will not want, but he who hides his eyes will get many a curse." God does not forget what you have done in love for others and He does not overlook it. (Hebrews 6:10) "For God is not unjust so as to overlook your work and the love that you have shown for His name in serving the saints, as you still do."

He warns us that if we do not help others, He may not help us. For He has mercy for the poor and we should also. (Proverbs 21: 13) "Whoever closes his ears to the cry of the poor will himself call out and not be answered."

When we do these things that we have been commanded to do and have been given the kingdom responsibility to do them, we uphold our obligation to the kingdom and its king. We please the king and when all is said and done, we will receive our rewards for the good that we have done and lose rewards for things we did not do. This is in reference to what you have read about in chapter 2 when I was talking about "The Judgement Seat Of Christ."

Now all of this we have talked about so far is about being under the Reign of a Righteous King (Jesus). He is the King of The Kingdom Of God. His Power, His Anointing, His Authority, and His way of doing things here on earth.

The Kingdom Of God is the kingdom of light, eternal, both in time and space. His kingdom is from eternity to eternity. His kingdom is legal. The whole universe was created by God and it belongs to Him and He has the legal right to Reign over it.

There is unfortunately another kingdom, the kingdom of Satan. There is a spiritual warfare going on between the two kingdoms. The kingdom of Satan is the kingdom of darkness, this kingdom is not eternal in regard to time and space, it is limited in time and as to space, it is limited to the air and the earth. This kingdom is not a legal kingdom, it was established by a rebellion against God.

The Lord Jesus once called Satan "the prince (ruler)of the world." (John 14:30) and this reveals that Satan not only has a kingdom but also reigns over that kingdom. This kingdom is not under the reign of a Righteous King as it is in The Kingdom Of God, but is under the reign of an evil one, the Prince of Darkness. It is a counterfeit of God's kingdom.

Just as The Kingdom Of God has messengers of various ranks, His Angels, so it is also with Satan's kingdom. He has the angels that followed him out of heaven in rebelling against God. These are the principalities, powers, rulers, dominions, and the spiritual hosts of wickedness of the air, and Satan being the head and in charge of all of it. We are told about this in (Ephesians 6: 12, and 2:2 and 1:21)

Both of these kingdoms are spiritual kingdoms and they are not imaginary, they are not political, and they are not geographical, they are real kingdoms. And they are worldwide and one or the other exists in the hearts of all the people and every person belongs to one or the other of them.

As I said before, it is a counterfeit kingdom, but it is just as real as The Kingdom Of God. Those who belong to it are citizens of that kingdom. Satan counterfeits God in many things, but we will not get into that now because it would take another whole chapter to show and explain these things.

It was not my intentions to include this information about this kingdom of Satan into this chapter. However, I feel like I was led by the Holy Spirit to include it for the reason of pointing out some of the main differences between the two kingdoms and how the consequences of a person's choice can determine the type of life they can have here and now and also in their eternal life.

I suppose one of the easiest ways to do this is to have some type of comparison chart showing some of the differences and then a brief summary of the information along with maybe some questions or scripture from the Word of God. So here goes it. Bear with me. I do not want to spend a lot of time on this other than to get that info on paper that the Holy Spirit wants us to see.

Kingdom Of God		Satan's Kingdom Of Darkness
King	Jesus(Righteous King)	Satan (An evil Prince)
Realm	Heaven	Earth
Citizens	Saved Born Again Believers	Unbelievers and the Lost

Kingdom Of God		Satan's Kingdom Of Darkness
Law	The Gospel and Grace	Lies and Deception
Custom	Loving and Righteous	Hateful and Destructive
Power	Our Faith and Authority	Illusion and Theft
Authority	God Owned and God Given	Stolen from Mankind
Our Defense	God and His Delegated	Authority Absolutely None
Faith and Hope	In God, His Love, and Promises	Absolutely None
Restoration	Redeemed by the Blood of Jesus	None, only more Theft
Health	Healed by the Wounds of Jesus	Sickness, Disease, Death
Our Peace	Peace with and the Peace of God	Stress, Worry, Anxiety
Leadership	Helpful, Life Giving, Blessing	Kills, Steals, and Destroys
Our Life	Eternal with Love and Peace	Eternal Torment
Destiny	Paradise and Heaven	Torment and Hell

Well maybe this is enough comparison to show how much better God's kingdom is than that of Satan's. Not only your eternal life will be determined by the choice one makes about whom they will serve but also their life and quality of life they live here and now.

If you are saved and born again, rejoice and be glad. But if you are not, this chart should show the difference God can make in your life. The things mentioned on the chart are by all means not everything, but they should bring the things mentioned to your attention and show how much more God has to offer and how much better it would be to spend eternity with Him.

These words referring to this chart and the comments made here are not meant to be a scare tatic nor or they meant to judge anyone in any way. They are simply true and they are all according to the Word of God.

If you are not saved or you are not sure and you need help making a decision on this, if you have not already, here are some questions to consider.

1. Do I believe and acknowledge Jesus is my Saviour and Lord, or am I by default allowing Satan to rule over my life?
2. Am I a true believer in Jesus Christ and a citizen of His kingdom or am I among those of an unbeliever and a citizen of Satan's kingdom?
3. Is it a habit in my way of life to show the light and Spirit of Christ in my daily conduct or am I walking in darkness and fleshy desires?
4. Do I feel the desire and try to make it a priority to obey the teaching of Jesus or am I one who is deceived and disregard the importance of this covenant with God?

5. Am I living in the power and victory of Jesus, am I trusting and depending on God's Promises and His Grace, or am I living in my own weakness and failure deceiving myself and under the illusion that I am strong?

6. Do I have a genuine love for God and truly want Him to be a part of my life and have fellowship with Him or do I still do my own thing and give God a backseat in my life?

7. What is my destiny? Have I secured life after death? that eternal life in a heavenly glory with Christ, or will I be cast away into everlasting torment and eternal punishment?

These are very important questions and they all really need to be considered seriously and with honesty.

If you still have not asked Jesus to be your Saviour and Lord and have not received your salvation and been born again, and after considering what you have just read and you desire to do this, remember the prayer of salvation that is on page 17 in this book and go and pray it out loud now and mean it with all your heart.

If you have prayed it already and meant it with all your heart and you have found something in the list of questions just asked that you are not sure of and feel a little uncomfortable about and have that desire to do something about it, be blessed for that is the conviction of the Holy Spirit. He will help you overcome whatever it is if you will give Him freedom to work in your life. Ask God to help you with whatever it may be and He will.

Now let me make one thing perfectly clear, if you are being convicted by the Holy Spirit, He is very precise and right on target about what He is convicting you about and He does not try to confuse you. If you are feeling anything other than that, it is not the Holy Spirit. If you are feeling confused or if you are having a numerous amount of thoughts of guilt or condemnation, that is from Satan. Dismiss those feelings, submit yourself to God, rebuke the devil, and He will flee from you.

Remember, we are under Grace and not the Law. We are Righteous because of Jesus. God is faithful and just and will forgive us our sins when we confess them to Him. He forgives us, cleanses us from all unrighteousness, and forgets our sin. Do not, and I say again, do not let Satan condemn you, make you feel ashamned, or make you feel guilty for anything. You ask God to forgive you and receive your forgiveness, In Jesus Name.

I feel like this needed to be said so that you who were concerned about the list of questions would have peace and not be worried about anything because God does not want you to be worried or upset but wants you to have peace.

I got a little off track in this writing but I felt led by the Holy Spirit to say this to you who were concerned about the list so that you would know what you were feeling.

Now let us get back on track and briefly recap what we have just read about the two kingdoms. In short, it is plain to see that The Kingdom Of God is a much better place to be. And in it, is the true power and hope we need to have victory in our life.

So in summary, you can see how many rights we have in The Kingdom Of God, but let me remind you that all of these rights are only made available to us by the Blood of Jesus and by the Grace of God and us accepting Jesus as our Saviour and King and becoming a born again believer.

Being a member in God's Family and being a child of God also gives us even further rights and blessings. But it is not just all about our rights and our blessings, it is also about our responsibilities as a citizen of the kingdom and as children of God.

God is merciful to us because He loves us so much and He wants us to love others just as He loves us. We are to show that love to others and help others so that we can bring Him Glory and to be obedient to His command.

We need to be always thankful to God for what He has done for us and always honor and reverence Him because He is worthy of all Praise and Glory. He has sacraficed so much for us, His only Son, and we should never take that for granted.

We should not grieve or quench His Holy Spirit that lives in us or never take Him for granted either. We should honor His Presence with us and always respect and reverence Him as well, for He is God the Holy Spirit.

As I said before, God's Grace, this unmerited favor, that He has given us as a gift makes these rights available. We do not deserve any of these things that He has given us because of anything we have done and we certainly could not earn them. So let us always have a grateful heart toward God and do our best to please Him and to be the person He wants us to be.

He has invested so much in us, and we have been bought with a high price by the ultimate sacrafice and the precious Blood of Jesus and He does not want to lose us over to Satan and his kingdom. That is why He made His authority available to us so that we could use it against Satan and not be vulnerable or defeated by Satan and all his deception and destruction.

That is what the next chapter is going to be about, Our God Given Authority. I urge you to take this chapter and the remaining chapters of this book seriously and get the content of it deep down into your spirit for it will truly change your life.

CHAPTER 5

USING OUR GOD GIVEN AUTHORITY

Now this chapter may seem to some as a little bit radical because it is not taught in many churches and may even get you kicked out of some, but it is the Word of God and we will see that as we read and study this chapter.

It may also seem to make prayer look like it is not important but that is not true. Prayer is very important and we should never ever stop praying because it is our communication and our lifeline to God our Father in Heaven.

There is power in prayer and promises from God to answer prayer, especially if it is in accordance to His Will, and that is why it is important to know what the Will of God is.

Knowing God's Will helps us in our prayer life. It helps us and leads us to pray the right way and the right type of prayer. There are many different types of prayer and each one is important and each one of them requires us to have the knowledge and the understanding of how to pray that particular prayer.

Now this is not to say that God won't hear you when you pray any prayer, it is only to say that it is helpful and may get a quicker response if you pray it knowing His Will and Promises concerning that particular prayer and speak that promise as you pray. God does not forget His Promises and He is faithful to honor the Promises that He has made.

As I have said there are many different types of prayer and I will mention some of them briefly because I want to get into this chapter about our God given authority.

And I will say again that I am in no way saying that prayer is not important because it is vital in the life of a believer. We should pray everyday and we should talk to God frequently during the day and night acknowledging that He is present with us.

Jesus prayed to the Father a lot and so should we. So by all means keep praying because He is our Father in Heaven and our best friend. If you have a friend here on earth and stop talking to them, it is very likely that the friendship won't last and will come to an end, so it is also with our prayer life and fellowship with God. Keep praying and talking to God and stay in fellowship with Him.

I will explain shortly what I meant when I made the statement about it may seem like prayer is not important, but right now let us briefly look at some of the prayers I have mentioned and a little information about each one.

Now these are just a few different types of prayers and not all of them. They are just a few examples of the different kinds of prayers we pray and the things you may need to know to pray them.

The Prayer Of Salvation

A person prays this type of prayer when they come to realize they need a Saviour and accept and acknowledge Jesus as their Saviour. I have included this prayer in this book in chapter 2 for anyone who needs to pray it. This prayer requires no special understanding or knowledge, other than realizing that they need a Saviour, it only needs to come from the heart and sincerely meant and God will answer it.

The Prayer of Thanksgiving

Pretty much self defined. It is a prayer of giving thanks to God for what He has done for us and what He is doing for us. We should always have a grateful heart and let God know that we are thankful for all He does, even for all the little things that He does. For this is the Will of God. (1 Thessalonians 5: 16-18) This is a prayer from the heart with true gratefulness and sincere thankfulness to God for what He has done.

Prayer Of Faith or sometimes called The Prayer Of Petition

This is one particular prayer that you need to know what the Will Of God is concerning that prayer before you pray it. Find out what His Word says about the request you are making in your prayer, know His Promise or Will concerning it, and pray according to the promise. Write it down if you wish, and pray according to what His Word says and speak it in your prayer as you pray.

Prayer Of Intercession

A prayer where you pray for others for their requests, their needs, their help. You pray for them on their behalf. However, when you do pray these prayers it is important to know that your prayer will line up to the Will of God and His Promises.

Prayer Of Agreement

A prayer where two or more touch and agree and praying for the same thing or the same request and are in agreement for the same results of the prayer. Again, it must be in accordance to God's Will and Promises. (Matthew 18:19)

Prayer Of Consecration

This is a prayer of dedication, or a prayer of doing God's Will, or to be set apart by God for His purpose. This is a prayer where you will say "If it be your will." You may feel that you want to do something for God or have been called by God to do something like preach, teach, or have some form of Ministry. You pray your request and if it be God's Will that you do it, then so be it, if not, pray that He shows you His Will for your life and your calling.

Prayer Of Committment

A prayer of committing a person or circumstance to God. Releasing a burden to God and walking in obedience to His Word. Casting your cares upon Him. (1 Peter 5:7) It is important to remember that once you have prayed this prayer and given your problem to God, trust Him to work it out, stop worrying about it, be patient, don't take the problem back, don't pray the same prayer again, but instead continue to give thanks to God for Him working out the problem for you. And above all things, keep the faith and do not ever doubt, especially when Satan comes and tries to deceive you and convince you that nothing is happening. Trust in the Lord and lean not to your own understanding. (Proverbs 3: 5-6)

Prayer In The Spirit

Speaking and praying in tongues, a heavenly language, the tongues of angels. It is a language that the Holy Spirit prays through us and He speaks through us directly to God. We may not understand what is said, but God does. Some people do not believe in this and they do not do it because it requires them to yield of their voice to the Holy Spirit as He gives them utterance, but that does not change the fact that it is a real language and in the Word of God and is spoken of in many places. The Apostle Paul talks about this in the (1 Corinthians 14: 2-40) It is also believed that praying in the Spirit is praying in the power of the Spirit, by the leading of the Spirit, and according to His Will. The Holy Spirit also is called "The Helper" The Holy Spirit will help us to pray when we do not feel like praying, He will activate our desire to pray when we are discouraged or weak in our faith or do not know what to pray for. He will pray for us and make intercession for us. (Romans 8:26-27) To pray in the Spirit will require yielding to Him so that He can help us to pray.

Worship Prayer

Our Worship prayers are prayers of Adoration and Worship to God. We acknowledge our dependance on Him for all things. We thank Him and we exalt Him for all of His Greatness. We thank Him for His Faithfulness. We praise Him for who He is. We honor Him and offer up our sacrafice of praise to Him for He is worthy of all our praise. We worship Him in truth and in spirit for that is what is pleasing to Him. (John 4: 23-24) and He deserves all of it.

Now as I have said there are many different types of prayer and I have now only mentioned a few of them, and all of them are important, especially the prayer of salvation. However, my meaning in the opening paragraph of this chapter about prayer, is not that it is unimportant, but sometimes we may be asking God for something in prayer that He has already provided for us and He has already given us the authority to deal with it ourselves.

God's plan for us, and Him sending His Son to die for us, and all the things Jesus suffered for us, before and during His crucifixtion, has provided all the need required for us to receive our salvation, our healing, our peace, and all the things we need to have an abundant and happy life.

And what Jesus did between His death on the Cross and His Resurrection when He went to Hades and stripped Satan of his power and authority and taking the keys to death and Hell and the grave away from him, and then later Jesus delegating that same authority to born again believers, has provided us and has equipped us with the power and authority over Satan and all his evil.

This includes our God given authority that Jesus gave us over Satan's demonic activity and the sickness and disease that Satan puts on people. It includes our peace, our prosperity, and everything in our life that Satan has stolen from mankind at the time of human creation.

Jesus gave us that authority in (Luke 10:19) "I have given you authority to trample on snakes and scorpions and to overcome all the power of the enemy, and nothing will harm you." Now He said this to His Disciples but He has also delegated that same authority to us as born again believers, And I will show this to be true shortly as we study this according to the Word of God.

The snakes and scorpions in Luke 10:19 as we have just read pertains to and they represent the spiritual powers of Satan, the principalities and powers, and all his emissaries. The trampling on is referring to an ancient custom that when the kings and rulers of old time were defeated in battle, they were brought before the conquerer and the captains and the men of war so that they could put their feet on the neck of the defeated king before the king was killed.(Joshua 10: 24-25)

When Jesus had sent out the seventy in His Name to cast out demons and heal the sick that it talks about in Luke 10, they were amazed at what they had done. They were amazed of the healings that took place and by them using the name of Jesus that the demons obeyed them when they commanded them to leave someones body.

The authority and power that He gave them did not end with them, it is available to us today as born again believers as well. Jesus said this in (Mark 16: 17-18) "And these signs shall follow **those who believe**. In my name they will cast out demons; they will speak with new tongues; they will take up serpents; and if they drink anything deadly, it will by no means hurt them; they will lay hands on the sick, and they will recover."

Jesus was telling His Disciples this just before He ascended into Heaven. Now Jesus was not telling us to go out and handle snakes or to drink poison or to do anything to tempt or test God. He was promising us of His protection from the evil spirits when we are doing these things that He calls us to do. He is particulary watchful over those He has commissioned to do these things.

Casting out demons could be a dangerous thing but He has given protection to those He has called to do it. He has given them the authority to cast out the demons of oppression, of infirmity, of diseases and sickness, of all kinds of afflictions, and of all kinds of perversions. And He has promised protection to those that do it in His name.

Notice Jesus said in this verse, "signs shall follow those who believe" well that pertains to the believers of today just as it did to the believers of that day.

When Jesus and His Disciples were at what is called, The Last Supper, He taught them many things and among these things He was telling them about Him leaving and was going to be with the Father. He said He would ask the Father to send them another helper (The Holy Spirit). He gave them and us the commandment to love each other and told how the works that He did, that they and us can do also.

Jesus said, (John 14: 12) "Most Assuredly, I say to you, he who believes in Me, the works that I do he will do also, and greater works than these he will do, because I go to My Father."

Notice Jesus said, "he who believes in me" well that pertains to all believers, past, present, and future. And notice He said, "and greater works than these he will do because I go to My Father." He had just told them how the Father was going to send them the Holy Spirit, and a few verses later, He told of how the Spirit will dwell with them and be in them forever.

It is the power of God working in us by His Holy Spirit that produces the power for us to do anything. The reason He said "and greater works than these" is because His Holy Spirit today is in all true born again believers and He is in many more places at the same time doing those works. The Spirit had not been given to anyone like He has been today because Jesus had not been glorified yet. (John 7: 38-39)

We must know and understand as born again believers this power and authority that we have been given. When we speak, we must speak in faith, we must speak with our authority, we must walk in our authority, and we must know of our authority that God has given us.

We know and accept that wonderful work Jesus did for us on the Cross and we are so thankful for what He has did for us. We are also held responsible for much more. It is God's Will for us to be in good health, live a happy and prosperous life, have peace and joy, and have that abundant life Jesus came for us to have. Everything that Satan has stolen from us, we have the right to take it back. It is our responsibility to use this God given authority to take it back and not allow Satan to steal from us any longer.

Satan tries to steal our health, our finances, our peace, and all of these things just mentioned that is God's Will for us. That same authority that Jesus has is on the inside of us. We are in Christ and He is in us. You have to know that He has delegated that authority to us, and say it, use it, believe it, and stand on it for it to happen.

It is in the name of Jesus, and in His name only, that we are to use this God given authority. It is in our faith in believing, truly believing, that He will work through us by His Holy Spirit to do the work that He wants us to do for it to be successful.

When we enter into spiritual warfare with Satan and his demons, we are to know what the Word of God says about our authority, our victories, our indentity in God's Family, what the Will of God is, His Promises, and our rights as believers and children of God.

All true believers that have been born again in God's Holy Spirit have this authority given to them by God's Grace and our faith in believing it, truly believing it, and by us doing it.

Now there are many different gifts of the Spirit that are given to different believers for different things. All these gifts are important for they are needed for the body of Christ to be complete. Paul tells us of these gifts in (1 Corinthians, 12th chapter) He tells us that all the gifts are by the same Spirit and that all the different ministries are by the same Lord and it is the same God who works them all.

These are the gifts of the Word of Knowledge, Word of Wisdom, Faith, Gifts of Healing, Working of Miracles, Prophecy, Discerning of Spirits, Different kinds of Tongues, and the Interpretation of Tongues. There are other gifts as well, but I want to put the emphasis on healing.

We can all sing or dance, but some people are more gifted than others with special talents to sing or dance better than others. And just because we are not as gifted as someone else, it does not mean that we should never sing. So it is also with our God given authority that we have. God has given us all who truly believe and have His Spirit living in us the authority to call forth healing and the power of His Spirit manifest that healing. And just because we may not have that special anointing from God for the Gift of Healing does not mean that we should not use our God given authority given to us by Jesus for the purpose of healing.

Those big name entertainers and famous singers have a special talent and ability to do it. Those anointed by God for the Gift of Healing also have a special talent and ability to do it as well. But just because we do not have a big named famous healing ministry does not mean that we cannot use our authority given to us by the same God and the same Spirit to do it as well.

We are also commanded by Jesus to do this. In Mark 16: 17-18 that I mentioned earlier, about signs shall follow those who believe, the preceding verse, verse 15, says that Jesus commanded us to do this in His name as we are preaching the gospel. Now Jesus would not command us to do something if He had not equipped us to do it. Also remember what Luke 10:19 says "I give you the authority" Jesus delegated that authority to us as a born again believer and a citizen of His Kingdom.

Remember what I have said about the Kingdom Of God and Satan's kingdom in chapter 4, both of these kingdoms work by spiritual laws. Your faith and your authority are spiritual laws. Satan has to obey our gift of faith that we received from God and that authority that Jesus gave us when **we speak** the Word Of God using our faith and not doubt and believe that what **we say** will manifest in our lives. We have **to speak** that faith and authority into existence and we have to **say it** in order for it to manifest in both the spiritual and physical world. Believing it is not enough.

When we use that gift of Faith, it must be strong in a believer and they should have no doubt in their mind whatsoever if they expect to get results from the **words they speak** when using their authority. Also when we lay hands on someone for healing and their deliverance, if your faith is not mixed with love, it will not work. Love is a very strong requirement to be mixed with faith in order to be effective. You can have all faith and no love and it will not produce results. You can have many gifts of the Spirit, but if they are not mixed with love, they are not effective and they will be unprofitable. Paul said in (1 Corinthians 13: 1-2) "Though I speak with the tongues of men and of angels, and have not love, I am become as a sounding brass, or a tinkling cymbal. And though I have the gift of prophecy, and understand all mysteries, and all knowledge, and though I have all faith that I can remove mountains, and have no love, I am nothing." I think this scripture pretty much tells us how important it is to have love mixed with your faith and your gifts of the Spirit in order to be effective. It will not work without it.

God is love, and if we are to perform His Will and His operations here on earth, we have to operate in love. Jesus had love and compassion on those that He healed. He had Love and Authority and His Faith all working together. And you know what else? He had the same Spirit working in Him that we have in us. Christ is in us, and we are in Him.

People were healed by Jesus in many different ways. He touched some, sent out His Word on others, people who had faith touched Him, and He commanded even other healing by His spoken word. And in all of these healings that Jesus performed, it was God, who is love, who did it through His Holy Spirit that was in Jesus.

Now understand what I am about to say and do not misinterpret it. Jesus is 100% God, and He still was when He walked on earth during His Ministry. He walked as a man with a human body, just as we are. And because of God's plan for us to receive our redemption and salvation and to be reconciled back to Him and to take back from Satan the authority that was stolen from man at creation, Jesus had to become a man and made flesh. He was tempted in all ways just as we are, yet He had no sin. He only said and did what His Father said and had Him do and He was led by the Holy Spirit Of God that was on the inside of Him, the same Spirit we have inside of us.

However, Jesus walked in the fullness of the Holy Spirit yielding Himself completely to the complete obedience to the Father. He was a human man on the outside, but He was God on the inside.

Now we are not Jesus, there is only one Jesus, and there will always only be one Jesus. However, we are like Jesus was when He walked on the earth as a man, with the exception that Jesus was sinless and He had no need of salvation as we have needed. He was the God Man sent from God Himself from above who did not have a sinful and fallen nature as we once had. He was tempted just as we are, but He did not sin because He was able to walk in the fullness of the Spirit in a continuous and obedient way.

When we got saved, our sins were forgiven and we were put in right standing with God because of the Righteousness of Jesus. We became the Righteousness Of God In Christ because of what Jesus did for us and the Blood that He shed for us before and during the Cross. We became a new creation created in the likeness of Jesus, and adopted children of God, and became a citizen of God's Kingdom. We walk in human form as a spirit being just as Jesus did, but we still have that same body and soul our (will, mind, emotions) that we had before our new spiritual birth and that is why it is difficult for us to walk in the fullness of the Spirit in a continuous way as Jesus did.

We have trouble and we earnestly want to be able to completely yield ourself over to the leading of the Holy Spirit, and we strife to be able to do it, yet we can not do it on a continuous basis. However, we can be led by Him when we yield ourself over to Him and give Him the freedom to work in our lives.

God knows the desires of our heart and our weaknesses and strengths. And that is why when we mess up, He has promised us, that when we confess our mistakes, He forgives us and He puts us back in right standing with Him. I have said it before and will say it again, it is only by The Grace Of God that we receive anything from God and can do anything for God.

It is by this Grace that we are filled and anointed by God through His Spirit to do these things that Jesus told us to do. And if anointed, we walk in the power of His Spirit to do the things God has for us to do, and we do it in the Authority of Jesus' Name.

If you have received the Gift of Healing, you will walk in that anointing, and you will have that anointing readily available to you at all times. If you have not been given this Gift of Healing as a specific anointing, there can still be a healing manifested by the power of His Holy Spirit working in you. By you using your faith and by you **speaking** God's Word into the spiritual and physical world, this spiritual law of Faith will take dominion over that need of healing which you or someone else needs.

And remember, there can be no doubt or unbelief. You must be confident and stand firm in your faith. Pure, simple, childlike faith and **Bull Dog Strong**. Remember Jesus has already made that healing available to us by His stripes, wounds, and suffering.

We are to go by faith, not our feelings, not by what we presently see, but all by our faith. We are to **speak it out of our mouth** with confidence and no doubt. We are to **speak it** with our God given

Authority, we are to speak it in Jesus' Name, and we are to expect to get the results that we **have spoken** and **are speaking.**

Some healings manifest immediately and some do not, but that does not mean that the healing did not take place. Continue in faith and thank God for the healing every day. Claim and receive that healing, and believe in your heart with no doubt that you received that healing when you first **spoke it**, for as long as it takes, until you see it manifest in your life or the life of the someone you layed hands on in faith.

Understanding Spiritual Law will help us to believe and have faith in that what we say will manifest in our lives. These things I have already mentioned does not only pertain to the healing of sickness and disease, it also pertains to all things that God has promised us and wants us to have that Satan is trying to steal from us or trying to afflict us with.

We know from understanding God's Word, that it is not His Will for us to be sick or to not have peace in our lives. We know that He does not want Satan to steal from us and take those things that are rightfully ours.

By the promises God has made in His Word and believing and understanding how these spiritual laws work and this spiritual authority Jesus has delegated to us, God has equipped us with the means of keeping Satan from stealing things from us and trying to cause destruction in our lives.

Satan can not take possession of anything that is rightfully ours that God has given us through His Grace unless we surrender them to him. As believers, Satan has no authority over us but rather we have authority over him. And Satan knows this.

Satan uses all kinds of different ways and methods to deceive all people, both the believers and the unbelievers. We can open ourself up to him and give him an open door to interfer in our lives by being tricked by his deception and having a lack of that God given knowledge.

Knowing God's Word with His instruction and His Wisdom and His Promises will help us and give us the wisdom we need to stand against Satan. Knowing that we have this God given Authority over Satan and all his evil and using it and **speaking it** with faith will keep him from interferring in our lives.

He will come, you can count on that, and when he does we will be better equipped and prepared to defeat him.

My brothers and sisters in Christ, I encourage you to learn and study the Word of God for yourself and be not ignorant of how powerful it is when it comes to fighting off Satan and all of his spiritual forces.

That is the way Jesus fought him and that is the way we are to fight him also.

Remember your indentity in God's family, remember who you are, remember the authority that has been given to you as a citizen of The Kingdom Of God, remember the promises of God, and also remember the power of the words **you speak.**

Put on that Whole Armor of God that the Bible tells us about in Ephesians 6 and along with all of this, standfast and unmovable against Satan and all of his forces.

You truly do have authority over Satan and all of his emissaries, but you really need to be careful about the words you speak out of your mouth.

There is real power in your words. Just as your God given and healing words that you speak into the spiritual and physical world produce good and healing results, so it is also with your negative, doubtful, unbelieving, faithless, and careless words. They will produce negative and destructive results. They will produce the result that **you speak.**

Now what I am about to say may seem to some as a very radical statement, but it is a fact. These 2 worlds, the spiritual and the physical, have laws that govern them. The spiritual world has more dominance over the physical world and complies with what is spoken into it. You can see this when God spoke this physical world into existence. Remember "God is Spirit" (John 4:24) We are a spiritual being. Remember God is Spirit and when He breathed life into man at his creation, He breathed mans spirit to life (Genesis 2:7). And Jesus said to His disciples when He was telling them that He was the Bread of Life in (John 6:63) that the words He spoke to them were spirit. The words we speak as a spiritual being are spirit and they go forth into the spiritual world and physical world as we speak them.

Remember I said in chapter 1 when we talked about our spirit is who we are. We are a spiritual being whether we are born again or not. We have a physical body to house this spirit while we live in this physical world but our bodies are not who we are. Remember I said that your spirit is what lives forever and you have that choice by your decision of where it will go for eternity. If you are not saved, you still are a spirit and you are dead in your sins and seperated from God. If you are saved, you still are a spirit and have been reborn and brought to life and have been delivered from the law of sin and death. A spiritual law in the spirit world.(Romans 8:2)

As I said, this may seem to be a radical statement, but it it true and hopefully will give you an understanding of how these spiritual laws work in both worlds.

Do you remember in the Bible where it tells us about when Peter walked on the water when Jesus called for him to do so (Matthew 14: 25-31). This defied the law of gravity and the law of density. The law of faith in the spiritual law had dominion over the laws of gravity and density in the physical law.

Jesus cursed a fig tree in (Mark 11:13-25). He did this to teach His disciples of how powerful their faith could be. The fig tree, which is part of the physical world, had to obey Jesus' faith, which is part of the spiritual world. Again the law of faith and the Word of God dominated the physical law. You can see this happening throughout the Ministry of Jesus. It is no different today than it was then.

Again I am saying that we are not Jesus, but we have the same resources that Jesus had when He walked as a man. We have the same God, the same Holy Spirit, the same spiritual laws, and the same Word of God working today as they were then.

Our words are powerful, especially when they have faith working with them. The Book of Proverbs tells us in many places about "the power of our words" and Jesus has stressed to us in His teaching about the importance and the power of our faith.

I know everything in us, our earthly mind, which is part of our soul and not our spirit is trying to tell us that this is foolish and not true. But remember what the Word of God says in (Romans 12:2) about renewing our mind and thinking on God's ways and His system of understanding and doing things compared to the worlds system and the way the world understands and does things. This is especially important when it comes to exercising our faith and understanding God's Word, the spiritual laws, the power of the Word of God, and how the Kingdom of God works.

Anyway I think you have gotten an idea of what I have been saying about spiritual law, the law of faith, and the power that God's Word has over all things.

Our faith is a gift from God. When we get saved and born again, we each receive the same measure of faith (Romans 12:3). That faith will grow in us as we learn and believe and hear and meditate on God's Word (Romans 10:17). That faith will grow in us when we see the Faithfulness of God working in our lives. It is our faith in God's Word and His Grace and that authority that has been delegated to us that help us to be an overcomer and to have victory in our lives.

And that is why it so very important that we should always be careful about the words that we speak and also the thoughts that we think.

Our words and our thoughts come to life in everybodys life, whether they are a believer or not. If they make negative comments and complain all the time, the things they are speaking will manifest in their lives.

You can speak blessings or cursing, life or death, good and evil, and power or weakness right out of your mouth.

As a believer, a true born again believer, this is also true. If you speak blessing or you speak healing or you speak restoration into your life and mix it with your faith and do not doubt in your heart and believe that what you speak will happen, it will manifest in your life.

If you speak negative things, unbelief, doubt, fear, or sickness and disease out of your mouth, that is what you will get. Be very careful with your words.

That is what the next chapter, chapter 6 of this book, is going to be about. The Power of Our Words.

I urge you to take this next chapter seriously and cautiously because the teaching about this and the emphasis stressed on the importance of it can have a powerful effect in your life.

CHAPTER 6

THE POWER OF OUR WORDS

If we are to live a successful and victorious life as believers, we must be careful about the thoughts we think and the words we speak.

Our words we speak and the thoughts we think could be one of the most difficult things that we have ever tried to control.

God tells us in His Word that our words have incredible power. He tells us that our mouth and tongue can keep us out of trouble. (Proverbs 21:23) "Whoever guards his mouth and tongue keeps his soul from trouble.)

You can talk trouble into your life by saying negative things, doubting your faith and speaking it out, and not believing what God said about it.

If you pray a prayer and know that it is God's Will and the answer to that prayer does not manifest to you immediately and you get impatient and begin to doubt and start saying things like, maybe, or I hope, or I guess it just wasn't meant to be, those things you have said will be the result you get.

You must mix your faith with the words you speak and believe that you will receive those things you are praying about.

If you were worried about something and that is what you prayed about, stop being worried and begin to thank God for Him answering your prayer even if you don't see anything happening.

Remember His promises and His commands, and His promise to answer your prayer. Jesus said in (Mark 11:24) "Therefore I say to you, whatever things you ask when you pray, believe that you receive them, and you will have them. Now this is His promise to us to answer our prayer. There are other verses as well, but this is pretty plain and understandable.

So when you pray, believe that your prayer will be answered, especially if you know that it is God's Will. Do not get impatient and start saying things that can effect the outcome of that prayer.

If you have cares and troubles, remember what He said in (1 Peter 5:7) " Cast all your cares upon Him because He cares for you.) and remember what He said about us guarding our mouth and tongue.

You must use Bulldog faith, just as a bulldog gets his hold on a bone and will not turn it loose, get a hold of and take root in God's Word and His promises and do not let them go regardless of what you see or feel. Believe and know God will do what He said and do not doubt, be patient, and trust God.

This is true with all things, all prayers, and all circumstances. Do not let Satan trap you with any of his deception or tricks that he uses by creating doubt, unbelief, or any other lie from him that will keep you from receiving from God the things God wants you to have.

When you speak doubt, unbelief, fear, or anything else that is contrary to the Word of God and His promises, you open the door for Satan to come in and work in your life and to cause you problems.

Remember what was said in chapter 5 about your authority. You truly do have the authority over Satan and he does not have authority over you unless you open the door and give it to him.

We all need help to overcome Satan and all his evil, and that is why, among many reasons, God has given us His Holy Spirit to help us to do it. The Holy Spirit works His power in us and through us to use that authority that Jesus has given us.

Satan will come after us any way he can to try to steal our peace, our faith, our health, our joy, God's Word in us, or even our indentity in God's Family. He tries to kill us and destroy us in any way he can by using his deception, his lies, and his tricks.

Oh, but Glory be to God, our Father in Heaven, He has not left us as orphans. He has adopted us into His Family, He is our Father, and He will help us fight the enemy.

It is our responsibility to learn God's Word, His promises, and His commands. It is our responsibility to use that authority that He has given us over Satan. And it is also our responsibility to allow His Holy Spirit to have freedom to work in our lives.

With the help of the Holy Spirit and us speaking God's Word, we are able to resist the devil and all his deception. By knowing God's Word, when Satan comes to kill and to steal and to destroy, we are more prepared to take control of him.

If Satan can not get us caught in his trap one way, he will try another, and then if that does not work, he will try another. And where some people are able to resist him time and time again by using God's Word and their authority against him, they fall short in realizing how Satan can use their careless words against them later.

They are successful time and time again in resisting him, but later, they are careless with their everyday words and open that door to the devil. They use these words in a completely unintentional way not realizing the effect that they have. These words may seem to be harmless but are very harmful in reality.

These words are words used in a normal everyday conversation with others about things going on in their lives, or likes or dislikes, finances, health, places they would like to go, or whatever the conversation may be about. These words can talk trouble into their life if used carelessly and they are clueless as to their effect.

Some examples of these words are, for example, a person has really had the desire to go somewhere, and they tell another person they are talking with "I have just been dying to go there" or they talk to themselves when they goof up and make a mistake while doing something, and they say "Oh, I'm just getting old and senile" or someone may be really annoying someone and they say to that person "You just make me sick" or "I am sick and tired of........." I think you get the meaning of what I am saying.

These words may seem harmless and of no effect. But Satan can use them against you to gain entry into your life by you opening that door to him by your words. He walks around looking for opportunities and waits for someone to do such things so he can jump right in and cause trouble. (1 Peter 5:8) "Be sober (self control) and be vigilant (watchful, or on the alert), because your adversary the devil walks about like a roaring lion seeking whom he **may** devour." I remember my English teacher pointing this out to me when I was a young boy and showing me the difference between can and may. She said **can** is you are capable of doing something without permission and **may** is seeking the permission to do something. That is what Satan does, he seeks permission by watching for us to make mistakes due to our carelessness and our unawareness and giving him an opportunity by opening a door to him to enter and to give us trouble.

We all know how words can effect us and have consequences in this physical world and we need to know how they can have effect us in the spiritual world as well.

Be especially careful when talking about a disease or sickness, a doctors report, a financial problem, or a family situation. **Speak the Promise** and not the problem. **Speak faith** and not fear. **Believe** and do not doubt. Use that "Bulldog Faith" and hold on to God's Word and Promises.

You can not have faith and fear at the same time. One cancels out the other. So choose faith in God's Word and hang on to it like that bulldog with the bone, and all fear will leave you and you will have peace and be able to think more clearly and have control over what you say. You will be able to speak out of faith and not fear which will lock down the door to Satan and keep him from interferring in your life.

Satan uses deception to bring offense and strife into a persons life, both believers and unbelievers. He tries to get them to become angry and get offended so they will say things they ought not say. He is trying to get them to open the door for him by the words they speak through their anger or feelings being hurt by the offense.

But let it go, forget about it, forgive them in your heart, and keep quiet. It is not worth losing your peace, losing your control to Satan, and giving your authority a back seat.

Satan is the reason for many arguments and fights. Particulary among married couples. They fight and argue with each other instead of fighting the real enemy. They say things they do not really mean and regret it later and they take the bait of Satan, hook, line, and sinker. They open the door wide open for him to give them more trouble in their lives.

Think about who is the real enemy and what he is trying to do. Rather than fight each other, unite together, and fight the real enemy. If you are saved and born again, use that God given authority to get Satan off your back and under your feet. If you are not saved, get saved, not only just for your eternity, but also for the situations just like this. Because if you are not saved, and have no fellowship with the Lord Jesus and God the Father, and His Holy Spirit, you have no God given authority over the devil and you are among the unprotected prey. **<u>Think on this</u>** !!!

For the decision to get saved is the most important decision you will ever make in your lifetime. Remember there is a prayer you can pray on page 17 if you want to pray it. But truly mean it with all your heart.

We got off the subject for a moment, but I feel that this needed to be said.

We need to guard our mouth and tongue and always be careful what we say for it can bring destruction into our lives. The Book of Proverbs has many things to say about this. (Proverbs 13:3) "He who guards his mouth preserves his life, But he who opens wide his lips shall have destruction."

When your emotions, for whatever the reason, gets in the way of your faith and your wisdom of God's Word, it could lead to destruction. If you let yourself get really upset and it causes you to not think clearly, it will effect the words you speak and cause you to be snared in the trap of the devil. And you will be snared by your own words. (Proverbs 6:2) "You are snared by the words of your mouth."

One definition of snare in the dictionary says "a thing likely to lure or tempt one into harm or error." Well that is exactly what takes place when we say things we ought not to say. Satan has baited the trap, we take the bait, and have opened the door for him to do his thing and interfer in our lives and given him authority.

If and when this happens, we need to repent very quickly to God and submit ourself to Him and resist the devil for the devil to flee from us. God is faithful and just to forgive us and put us back in right standing with Him and we regain our authority over Satan and he has to flee from us. (James 4:7) "Submit yourselves, then, to God. Resist the devil, and he will flee from you."

In this 4th Chapter of James' writing, he is speaking about the passions and desires that war within us and causes us to argue and fight among ourselves. He speaks about our pride and our selfishness and tells how God opposes the proud and gives grace to the humble. He is warning us that being worldly is putting us in opposition to God.

Satan uses these things as a validation for him to interfer in our lives along with our unintentional invitation to him with the careless words that we speak out of our anger, hurt, fear, or doubt and unbelief.

Satan uses our mistakes to try to gain entry into our lives and he waits for that opportunity from us because of our mistakes and carelessness.

It is a very hard thing for us to tame our tongue and keep ourselves out of trouble but being aware of the consequences and the power of our words is a good place to start.

We should begin to practice being careful about what we say and ask God to help us.

We should always be alert and to recognize the tricks of the devil and to overcome him with the God given authority words of our mouth. We have all made mistakes in the past and just because of them does not mean that it is too late to start fresh.

If you are having trouble controlling your words, I urge you to call upon the Lord and ask Him to create in you a new heart. A new heart where the negative and careless speech cease to exist. If unforgiveness is present in your heart, ask Him to help you to forgive others and to help you love others as He loves us.

Jesus said that out of our hearts our mouth speaks. (Luke 6:45) "A good man out of the good treasure of his heart bringeth forth that which is good; and an evil man out of the evil treasure of his heart bringeth forth that which is evil, for out of the abundance of the heart his mouth speaketh."

Jesus taught that out of the overflow of the heart the mouth speaks. He was teaching about the good and evil thoughts that get stored up in our hearts.

We can not change our thoughts on our own. Our thought patterns have been with us a long time. We need the help of the Holy Spirit to do it. We need Him to fill our hearts with love and compassion and His good fruits. We need Him to help us to transform our minds to think as God thinks and do things according to the System of God and not the system of the world.

It is the Holy Spirit who gets rid of the demonic powers and helps us to fight our battles and resist evil. We speak our words of God given authority using God's Word and the Holy Spirit backs us up with His power to accomplish the job.

The presence of the Holy Spirit is in us and the Word of God we speak with our God given authority and the power of the Holy Spirit working in us and through us makes the devil flee from us.

It is kind of like a traffic cop and we are the officer. He can not physically make a car stop or go, but the authority given to him is recognized by the drivers of the cars and they obey what he tells them to do. If they do not acknowledge the authority the officer has, there will be consequences to pay. Just as the drivers of the cars would be breaking the physical law by not obeying the police officer, it is the same with the spiritual law. If Satan does not obey the God given authority delegated to us by Jesus there will be consequences to pay. Satan also knows this, and that is why he will flee from us.

The police officer knows he has this authority and has the faith to administer that authority, and so it is also with us as believers. We must know that we have that authority and have the faith to administer that authority.

Satan knows he has no authority over us unless we yield it to him and that he must obey the words we speak when we speak the Word of God with our God given authority or he will have to deal with God.

This is why it is very important to speak the right things and know the authority that we have as believers that is attached to those words.

So in summary, just like the authorative words we speak and the power they have, so it is also with all the other words we speak as well. The power of words can help us or hurt us, bring blessings or cursing, life or death, healing or sickness, or good or evil. They do not have to be intentional or purposeful, they can be accidental or careless and still have the same effect.

Our thoughts and things stored up in the abundance of our heart can effect the words that we speak. Any unforgiveness, resentful feeling, selfishness, hate, hurt, anger, or any kind of negative thoughts. We need to turn these feeling and thoughts loose and let them go and not allow any thoughts of this type to ever linger or be stored up in our hearts and in our minds. Not only for the reason pertaining to our words we speak, but also because it hinders our fellowship with God and His Holy Spirit and His forgiveness and blessing for us.

Take root and ground yourself in the Peace of God, the Word of God, His Promises to us, in His Law of Faith, and fully trust God. By doing this, the world will not pull us back into its troubles, and the peace of God will keep our hearts and thoughts if we will keep our mind on Him and fully trust and rest in Him.

Paul tells us in the (4th chapter of Philippians), to think about pure and good things. He tells us not to get stressed out or to be anxious about anything, but for us to trust God and pray and to be thankful and let God know we need His help.

God already knows we need His help, but by us making our requests to Him, we have peace, the Peace of God, that surpasses all understanding, and this peace will guard our heart and our mind. (Philippians 4: 6-8)

This peace will help us not to sin when trouble comes and Satan tries to put us under pressure or to create fear in us. It will help us not to say the wrong things. It will help to keep us calm and not get stressed out.

If we will walk confidently and commit everything into the hands of God, and keep our mind on Him, He will keep us in perfect peace. (Isaiah 26:3) "Thou (God)will keep him in perfect peace, whose mind has stayed on thee (God): because he (us) trusts in thee (God)".

We have that peace through our Lord Jesus and the Blood that He shed for us. And by that Blood, He reconciled us to the Father, obtained our justification, obtained our righteousness through Him, made atonement for us, and made peace with God for us.

The unsaved person has no understanding of this peace and what this tranquility of the mind means. They suffer in their troubles and have many problems without this great quietness of the mind that God alone gives through Christ.

The unsaved person suffers many afflictions from the devil and has no authority over him to prevent him from interfering in their lives.

What an awlful and miserable life this must be. To have no control over their life and to be vulnerable to all the pain and suffering that Satan puts on them. If they only would realize that they needed a Saviour to save them from all of this.

If they would only realize that by not being saved, that not only their eternal life is in danger, but also that the quality of life that they live here and now could be so much better, more abundant, and more peaceful.

It was not God's plan for mankind for anyone to ever be lost and to have to suffer through this life and their life to come. When God created mankind, He gave them the dominion over the earth, but Satan stole it in the Garden Of Eden, and when God sent Jesus to restore that dominion to man and reconcile man back to God, it made all the difference and made these things available again to us.

I will ask once again, if you are not saved and have not been born again, please consider all of these things I have just said. If you are feeling that desire and the Holy Spirit is drawing you to Jesus and if you would like to get saved and born again, remember the Prayer of Salvation that is on page 21 of this book and go and pray it out loud now and mean it with all your heart and receive it by faith.

God wants us to be a voice for Him in this world, and that is why again, it is very important to be careful about the words we speak.

Our words need to be His Words, and the power of His Words need to be the power of our words. There is power in our words in all the things I have already mentioned and also in our words of testimomy and witnessing for Jesus.

We are all called to witness for the Lord, this you can be sure of, and when we go about witnessing for Him, His Holy Spirit works in us and in the people to whom we are speaking and causes them to be receptive to our words. He reaches into their heart and helps them to understand the words that we speak. He uses our words to soften the heart of those who are listening and He makes our words have power and meaning. He urges that person or persons to receive Jesus and get saved.

God has said that His Word would not return to Him void, but would accomplish that which He purposed it to do. (Isaiah 55: 10-11)

His Word should not return to us void either, we must believe it like He does. When we speak it, we must have the God like faith to see it accomplish what we purposed it to do. We must have no doubt and only believe that what we say will happen.

This is possible to do as you grow in your faith and get more and more results from the words you speak.

As we begin to talk right, walk right, and yield ourself more to God and the leading of the Holy Spirit, we will begin to notice and see how powerful our words truly are.

When a person begins to see who they truly are in Christ, it will change their life. They will understand their indentity in God's Family, the authority that He has given us, and the understanding of how the spiritual laws work with God's Word. They will see how powerful our words are, understand our citizenship in God's Kingdom, and will see God's love and favor for us. They will experience this great peace that God has for them. God's Grace will grow in them and their faith will grow in them. They will become a powerful and useful person to be used by God to show His Glory here on earth.

I hope that I have gotten the point across in this and the preceding chapters as to who we are in Christ and who He is to us. That we truly need Him and that He truly wants to be a part of our lives.

I hope that I have made it perfectly clear in this chapter of how the words we speak are powerful. And how they can bring us blessing or destruction, or can bring life or death, or can bring healing or sickness, or they can bring power or weakness. Be careful what you say and how you say it.

Study and meditate on God's Word and get it deep down into your spirit. Believe it with all your heart and then speak it out of your mouth with faith and watch things begin to change in your life.

Be patient and stand strong in your faith, never doubting or compromising the Word of God. Truly believe what His Word says and trust God to do His part as you obey what He has told us to do.

God is our only true hope in this life. We have tried on our own in the past and have so miserably failed. We have put our trust and faith in other people and have been so many times disappointed. Do not put your faith in mankind, but rather put your faith in God and His Word and settle it once and for all in your heart and in your mind to trust God and believe He will do exactly what He said He would do.

God is Faithful to His Word and to us. He will not allow us, as believers, to be utterly destroyed by Satan and all his evil. We should have no fear of Satan or any of his deception because God will protect us.

You should never fear but rather have faith in God and His Word. Fear opens the door for Satan to work in your life. Fear steals your peace and it prevents your faith from doing its work in your life. It contaminates your faith.

You can not have fear and faith at the same time. You will either have one or the other because one will cancel out the other.

If you truly trust God and have faith in Him and His Word, it is unlikely that fear will have any effect on you when Satan comes to kill, steal, and destroy.

Fear is a manifestation of the spirit world. The evil spirit world, because God does not want us to fear. You can not see it but you can feel it and you know that it is there. It is subject to and can be controlled by the spiritual law of faith just as all other things can be, and God's Word takes control over it just as it does over all other things.

The only fear that God speaks of is "the fear of the Lord" and this is not a fear as a meaning for us to be scared of or frightful of Him, but rather a meaning for us to reverence and show honor to Him.

Fear is what we are going to talk about in this next chapter, chapter 7, "Do Not Fear For We Have Hope" I urge you to read and meditate on it carefully and get these things deep down into your spirit. And when the enemy comes with his deception and lies and tries to create fear in your life, you will be better prepared to overcome him and maintain your faith and your peace. Remember the devil is a liar.

Remember in (John 8:39-44) when Jesus was talking to the Jews who said that they were the descendants of Abraham. Jesus told them "If you were Abraham's children you would do the works of Abraham. But you seek to kill me ....You are of your father the devil.............When he speaks a lie, he speaks from his own resources, for he is a liar and the father of it." Jesus called the devil a liar.

CHAPTER 7

HAVE NO FEAR FOR WE HAVE HOPE

Before I begin this chapter, I would like to again say, that it is only by the Grace of God, and the Blood of Jesus, and our faith, that we receive anything from God.

When I think of all the suffering and pain that Jesus went through for us and how much Him and the Father loves us, and how Jesus bore all of our sins, and all of our sickness, and all our diseases, and everything He suffered for our peace and abundant life, so that we would not have to, it really touches my heart.

I am so grateful and I will not disappoint my Heavenly Father and Jesus, my Lord and Saviour, by not receiving this wonderful and merciful gift. I will not allow fear and the other tricks and deceptions of the devil to enter into my life.

Jesus has paid it all in full, nothing else is due, so fear and all the other instruments that Satan uses has no right in my body. It is a violation of the covenant I have with my Father in Heaven and the promises He has made to me. Amen.

God has told us not to fear, for He is with us always. He has told us that He will not fail us, and He will not because He is Faithful.

There are at least 150 times in the Bible, from Genesis to Revelation, where God has told us not to fear. So I believe that He does not want us to fear.

Fear is a frequently used instrument used by Satan to try to get people to fall under his control. He uses fear to try and steal their peace, cause confusion, to create doubt, to get them to speak the wrong things, and to try and destroy their faith.

Anchor yourself in the Word of The Lord, be not deceived, take control, and do not fear. Be careful of what you do, say, and think regardless of what the situation is.

If you get a bad doctor report or you are having financial problems or you are in some sort of family crisis, take the Word of God and speak it and believe it and have faith in what you are saying.

Focus on the promises of God and do not focus on the problem. Speak to that problem using God's Word and His Promise, and speak to it with true faith and no doubt, and tell that problem to be gone, and do it in the authority of Jesus' Name. Then after all has been said and done, believe in what you said and give thanks to God for Him being faithful to His promise.

Do like Jesus did when He spoke to and cursed the fig tree and it had no fruit on it. He said to the tree (Mark 11:14) "Let no one ever eat fruit from you again." and then He turned and walked away and said nothing more, knowing that what He said would manifest, and the next day, the tree had dried up from the roots.

He did this as a lesson to His disciples who heard Him speak to the tree for the purpose of teaching them about how powerful their faith in God and their words they speak could be and about how the law of faith has supremacy over all other laws.

Later in the same chapter, Jesus tells them to have faith in God and about speaking to a mountain and telling it to move by using their faith and believe in what they say and not doubt in their heart and it would have to obey what they say.(Mark 11: 22-23)

He was teaching them about how the spiritual laws of the Kingdom of God works and the power of the Word of God. The Kingdom of God is a Spiritual Kingdom. It is the power, anointing, authority, and God's way of doing things. That understanding of His Kingdom is on the inside of us, and it is by and through His Holy Spirit.

Jesus said "have faith in God." and He also said "do not doubt in your heart but believe." It is possible for someone to have faith and still have unbelief in their heart. They have to get rid of that unbelief for that faith to work. It is not so much as how much or how big your faith is, it is rather having that small amount of unbelief and doubt that can keep your faith from working.

This doubt and unbelief is a result of our being conformed to this worldly system. We have been accustomed to this system for a long time. We have to truly renew our minds and conform our way of thinking to God's System and truly believe in His Word and His Spiritual Laws.

As we grow spiritually in God's Word, His Grace, and our faith, we will grow stronger as we see more and more results from our committment, and this unbelief and doubt will cease and we will see our faith and God at work in our lives even more.

When the disciples came to Jesus in Luke 17 and ask Him to increase their faith, Jesus told them the same thing about mountain moving faith except He was comparing their faith to the size of a mustard seed and using a mulberry tree as the example instead of using a mountain (Luke 17: 5-6).

Our faith is very important, we have to have it in order for us to believe, to trust, to depend on, and to please God. We must have faith to believe His Word and to believe in who He is and all of His promises.

No matter how bad the situation or how empty the feeling, we must use faith and rely on His promises. We must believe that He will never abandon us or leave us but will do that in which He has promised.

He will always be with us and help us when we need Him and there is no need to fear because all is well. He has not given us a spirit of fear. (2 Timothy 1:7) "For God has not given us a spirit of fear, but of power, and of love, and of a sound mind."

The more faith you have and use, the less likely it will be that you will have fear. You can not have fear and faith at the same time. I guess one way of saying this is, if you have faith, it is faith in God, and if you have fear, it is faith in Satan.

You can not have faith in both at the same time and neither would you choose to do this. We are to only have faith and worship God and to resist the devil. For the devil is our worst enemy, he is liar, a thief, and a murderer. There is no good in him and we should never trust him.

The more Word of God you hear and know and study and meditate on and get deep down into your spirit, the more faith you will have. Remember what the Word says in the Book of Romans. (Romans 10:17) "Faith comes by hearing, and hearing by the Word of God."

Think of the stories you may have heard about how powerful fear can be. A mother sees a car that is jacked up and her husband or son is under the car working on it and the car falls off the jack and on the person. She panics in fear, runs out and lifts the car off the person and frees them. Now if fear has that much power, think about how much greater power the law of faith in God can do.

When we truly understand and believe and know that God loves us, and He cares for us, and He will never leave us, we can be assured that we can trust and depend on Him for help when we call on Him.

He wants us to depend on Him and it pleases Him when we do. It gives Him the opportunity to prove His Faithfulness to us and pleases Him when we show our faith and trust in Him.

When we get to the point that we are not moved by what we hear or see, but rather we have put our whole being into trusting and believing God, we have entered into His Rest.

When we enter into the Rest of God, that peace and confidence will begin to dictate our life. If we keep our minds on Him and never compromise His Word and know that He is always with us, and believe it by faith, we will overcome the world.

The world and its troubles will be all around us, but we will not be moved because we are standing tall and believing in our faith and trust in God. He will give us perfect peace. (Isaiah 26:3) "You

(God) will keep him (us) in perfect peace, whose mind has stayed on you (God), because he (us) trusts in you (God)."

Jesus was talking to His disciples in John 14 and telling them that He would be leaving soon to go to His Father and He would ask the Father to send the Holy Spirit to them and to us to help us. He told them before He left that He would leave them and us His peace. (John 14:27) "Peace I leave with you. My peace I give to you, not as the world gives do I give to you. Let not your heart be troubled, neither let it be afraid." This peace that Jesus left us is unconditional peace, perfect peace, not like the peace of this world.

Jesus has given us His Peace, Our Father God keeps us in perfect peace, and one of the fruits of His Holy Spirit is peace. If we grab hold of this and keep our minds on God and believe and trust him, we will have this peace and we will walk in this peace.

All of these things I have mentioned in this chapter and all of the previous chapters about our authority, guarding our heart and mind, being careful about what you think and speak, they all work together

If we are to keep this peace that God has promised us, and not to have fear in our lives, we must remember of how important it is of all these things working together and our resposibility to make sure they do.

It is like a recipe in a book. If you leave out any of the ingredients, the end result would not be right. All the ingredients would be needed to have that perfect dish. So it is also with our perfect peace. You must use all of the information provided in order to have and maintain that perfect peace.

As I have said at the beginning of this chapter about fear being a tool that Satan uses against us to try to destroy our lives and to steal our faith, it begins as a thought and then creates emotion that can effect our thoughts and our speech. It becomes a strong intense feeling and that feeling can result in us making wrong decisions and saying and doing the wrong things.

When we learn to walk by faith and not by our feelings or by what we see, and not let fear or any other lie from Satan rule over our life, we will become overcomers. We will live that happy and that peaceful and satisfying life in Christ that God intended for us to do.

We must control our thoughts and not let fear ever be a part of our thoughts. Our thoughts can dictate who we are and can help us or hurt us. Your thoughts enter into your heart and you can be affected by what your heart or spirit is thinking.

When Jesus made the ultimate sacrafice and died for us and God the Father raised Him from the dead, all things that pertains to us in this life and our life to come was completed and taken care of, our salvation, our healing, our peace, our authority over our enemy, our being overcomers of this world, and our life of abundance.

When we got saved and born again and received His Holy Spirit into our lives, all these things were made available to us through our belief in Jesus and our faith in God and His Grace. So think on these things and always remember them.

Depression or anxiety or worry or fear should have no place in our hearts. When these feelings try to come, and they will, think on what the Lord Jesus and our Father God has already done and how they have already delivered us from these things.

Do not let these feelings of fear or any negative feelings linger or take root in your heart or spirit. They will affect who you are and the way that you think and the way that you speak. The Book of Proverbs tells us many things about this and how these thoughts can have impact on your life. (Proverbs 23:7) "For as a man thinks in his heart, so he is." You will become what you think, whether it be good or bad.

(Proverbs 12:25) "Anxiety in the heart of a man causes depression, but a good word makes it glad." Be careful what you allow to enter into your heart. God's Word is always a good encourager and prayer and your faith will overcome anxiety.

(Proverbs 15:13) "A merry heart makes a cheerful countenance, But by sorrow of the heart the spirit is broken."

As we study and learn and meditate on the Word of God, we will begin to receive the knowledge and understanding that God wants us to have. We will maintain that peace that God gives us and not get stressed out and not allow our spirit to be broken.

(Proverbs 17:27) "He who has knowledge spares his words, and a man who has understanding is of a calm spirit."

(Proverbs 17:22) "A merry heart does good like medicine, but a broken spirit dries the bones." A broken spirit can steal your joy, your health, and your faith. But a joyful heart or spirit can keep you and sustain you in all your ways.

Now by looking at this last scripture, it should give us the idea of how the condition of our heart, our spirit, can effect our health. Being stressed out, or depression, or fear, or hate, or anxiety, or unforgiveness in our heart can take us to an early grave.

Do not let Satan take you out because of any of these things. Stand firm in your faith and use your God given authority over him. Remember your identity in God's family and His promises and how much God truly loves you. And also be sure to remember how the Spiritual Law of Faith works and speak it with confidence and no doubt.

We are the children of God and He loves us, and His love is perfect, for God not only has love, but God is love. We can rest in this truth.

As we love one another as He has commanded us to do, God will abide in us, and His love that we will show others will be perfected in us. Because He has given us His Holy Spirit, God abides in us and if Him and His Word abide in us, we abide in Him.

It is His Spirit that helps us to develope that love and only in the path of love that this wonderful blessing can be found. It is only by the Holy Spirit that we are able to have it and to have that love perfected in us.

Now it is important to know that the word perfected used here, as some people may understand it, may seem to some as meanng something that had flaws and was made perfect and became flawless, but this is not the meaning used about this.

It is rather more of the meaning of completeness or finished or has obtained its goal. The word perfected could discourage believers into thinking that it is beyond their capabilities or an unreachable standard.

When our sacrafice of deep rooted obedience to God concerning His command of us loving one another and our free will and self-giving love to others is realized in the body of Christ, and to those who need to be led to Christ, God's love has obtained its goal and its purpose and its divine given intention.

If we seek to experience the love of God only for our own sake and not try to show His love that He has for others, we give the evidence that we do not truly know God and that we do not truly understand the Gospel of Grace.

God's love is extended and shared with us in order that we may imitate God and to show and share it with others. This is what God wants us and commanded us to do.

It is also to these people who do this, that God gives them the blessed and positive assurance that they are truly His children.

There are several dominate principles of human nature and fear and love are among them. If one takes control over the other, the other will cease to exist. They are opposite in nature and can not exist together at the same time. When one rises the other fails. If love shuts down and the light goes out, the tragedy of fear will come to life. This will open a door to Satan for him to interfer in your life.

God has told us in His Word that there is no fear in love. (1 John 4:18) "There is no fear in love, but perfect love casts out fear, because fear involves torment. But he who fears has not been made perfect in love."

If we are to be perfected in God's love, because God is love, we are to love others. If we truly love God, we truly love others. God has plainly said that we can not love Him if we do not love others. (1 John 4:20-21) "If someone says I love God, and hates his brother, he is a liar. For he who does not love his brother whom he has seen, how can he love God whom he has not seen. And this is the commandment we have from Him. That he who loves God must love his brother also."

So let us evaluate our love for others and see where we stand from God's point of view on our obedience to His Word. If we are somehow lacking in genuine and sincere love for others, pray and ask God to help us to love. Pray and ask God to help us to have the love He wants us to have, to help us to forgive others, and to put into us that heart of love and compassion for others.

So in summary, all of these things you have read about in this chapter is vital and is of an absolute necessity to us being assured that we can overcome fear. Everything that has been mentioned, our faith, our love, our peace, our thoughts, our words, and the recipe that we talked about, all need to be practiced and working together.

And among all these things, fully trust God and believe and never doubt. Study and learn and meditate on His Word and let His Word become a part of you. Be a doer of His Word and not a hearer only.

Put your faith into action by not only believing it, but also speaking it into existence. You have to speak it out of your mouth in order for it to engage its forces into both the spiritual and physical realm.

Talk the talk and walk the walk in a genuine, sincere, faith moving mountains type of way. Do not ever doubt or have the slightest amount of unbelief. Because if you do, it can affect the way your faith will work for you.

God knows your heart and your intentions and He will help you and establish you in all your ways if you will allow Him the freedom to work in your life. Remember, we truly do have hope, a true hope, and He is our only true hope.

If it were not for God, we would have no hope, we would be lost in our way. We would be in confusion, and we would be worried about things all the time. We would never be able to experience this perfect peace that He has given us as a gift.

We would have no authority over Satan and his destruction. We would spend eternity in eternal damnation. Our life here on earth would be full of misery and torment. We would never experience His unconditional love He has for us.

He fills the voids in our lives. He gives us strength when we are weak. He gives us the confidence and courage we need to stand firm in our faith. He will never abandon us or leave us destitute.

He is our Blessed Hope and our Rock. He is our protector and our foundation. He is our wisdom and our understanding. He is our forever present help. He is our peace. He is our God full of grace and mercy and love.

Glory to God, Blessed be the Name of the Lord, Glory and Honor to His Name.

"May our God and Father bless you richly and give to you, the ears, the eyes, and the mind, of His wisdom and understanding. May you receive these words deep down into your spirit and let God perform His work in you. And may you feel and experience the perfect and unconditional love that God has for you. I ask this for you in the Holy Name of Jesus. AMEN"

Thank you for taking the time to read this book. "Now receive it, in Jesus Name."

CONCLUSION

In summary of this book, it is not your everyday teaching that you will receive in a lot of churches. It is not about the religious do's and do not's. It is not about the act of self righteousness trying to make yourself right with God. It is not about the teaching that you have to do something for God first before He will do something for you. It is not about teaching that God brings sickness and trouble into your life to teach you a lesson or to get your attention.

It is about how we are truly made right with God and how it is by the Blood Of Jesus and God's Grace and His Faithfulness and His Love that we are put in right standing with Him. It is about how God truly loves us and what He has made available to us by the Blood Of Jesus and by His Grace. It is about the true Will of God in our lives and the power and authority He has given us to accomplish His Will. It is about God and His Promises that He has made to us.

This book is also about our responsibilty as a born again believer and our rights as a citizen of the Kingdom of God and as an adopted child of God. It is about how the law of faith in the spiritual realm can dominate all other physical and spiritual laws as the Lord Jesus taught during His Ministry here on earth.

In short, this book will help someone have that more abundant life that Jesus spoke of and was sent to earth as a man to make available to us.

It has been a priviledge and an honor to have the opportunity to write this book. I feel that not only has it been a blessing from God and an act of obedience to Him for me to do so, I also believe that it will be a blessing to anyone who may read it.

It was my intention to try to write things as clearly as possible and to try to explain the content with as much understanding as I could.

These words of teaching in this book are the true and Divine Word of God and they have been written under the direction and the inspiration of His Holy Spirit.

Feel free to read and confirm what has been written, as you should do anyway, and be open minded as you read and study it.

I truly and honestly believe that if you immersed yourself in the teaching in this book and study and meditate on the Word of God, it will surely change your life.